CAN I GET A WITNESS?

ESSAYS, SERMONS, AND REFLECTIONS

MERCER
UNIVERSITY PRESS

*Endowed by*
TOM WATSON BROWN
*and*
THE WATSON-BROWN FOUNDATION, INC.

# Can I Get A Witness?

ESSAYS, SERMONS, AND REFLECTIONS

## Bill J. Leonard

Mercer University Press
Macon, Georgia

MUP/ P479

© 2013 Mercer University Press
1400 Coleman Avenue
Macon, Georgia 31207

First Edition

Books published by Mercer University Press are printed on acid-free paper that meets the requirements of the American National Standard for Information Sciences—Permanence of Paper for Printed Library Materials.

Mercer University Press is a member of Green Press Initiative (greenpressinitiative.org), a nonprofit organization working to help publishers and printers increase their use of recycled paper and decrease their use of fiber derived from endangered forests. This book is printed on recycled paper.
ISBN       978-0-88146-468-9
Cataloging-in-Publication Data is available from the Library of Congress

*To Rose Marie Wallace Knudson, Erlene Henton Smith, Ila Henton Robinson, Mary Lee Daugherty, Sarah L'Heureux, Mildred Birch, Geneva Brown, Sue Coffman, Danetta Thornton Owens, Jean Gaskin, Pauline Cheek, Marilyn Dunn, and Patsy Ayers, women whose witness has been profound for me and all who know or knew them.*

# CONTENTS

# Preface

"Can I get a witness?" Our pastor, the Rev. Darryl Aaron, asks that question in almost every sermon he preaches at First Baptist Church, Highland Avenue, Winston-Salem, North Carolina. The question becomes especially poignant when he wants the congregation to join him in response to a specific gospel imperative. Answering his "call and response" on Sunday is relatively easy. Actualizing the gospel imperatives in daily life takes far greater courage.

As the twenty-first century muddles along, perhaps the phrase, "Can I get a witness?" will sharpen our thinking about the current state of religion in American culture, particularly for Protestants. Indeed, the permanent transition that characterizes American religious life offers an opportunity to revisit the word "witness" and its meaning for the future. For my seventeenth-century Baptist forebears, the idea of witness seemed inseparable from dissent—declaring who they were in a state-privileged religious culture that denounced and often harassed them as purveyors of a false gospel. That initial witness led them to insist that all church members must affirm a direct experience of God's grace and to resist the mandated baptism of infants, as well as allegiance to what they saw as a state-privileged church controlled by a ministerial hierarchy. Their "believers' church" was also something of a "peoples' church." One early confession of faith (1611) notes that believers "ought, when they are come together, to Pray, Prophecy, break bread, and administer all the holy ordinances, although as yet they have no Officers, or that their Officers should be in Prison, sick, or by any other means hindered from the Church."[1] (They apparently took it for granted that a Baptist witness would land their church "officers" in jail.) Quakers, too, took up a witness so public and profound that the Standing Order of New England Puritans sought to silence them with imprisonment and death. So Quaker Mary Dyer was hanged in Boston in 1660 because she would not keep her gospel to herself.

Revivalistic Protestants often used the word witness to describe their evangelical and missionary duty to declare the gospel locally and

---

[1] William L. Lumpkin and Bill J. Leonard, *Baptist Confessions of Faith, Second Revised Edition* (Valley Forge PA: Judson Press, 2012) 111.

globally, from one-on-one evangelism to a worldwide mission strategy. Others, however, (Primitive and Strict Baptists, for example) believed that their witness was to uphold the sovereignty of the God who without need of human intervention would save those elected before the foundation of the world. The intensity of such diverse Protestant witnesses often led them to denounce each other as false churches outside the doctrinal or salvific boundaries of God's grace. Competing and contradictory views on the nature of the Christian witness abound in American Christianity. While diverse communions may claim a common commitment to the gospel of Christ, they differ considerably on its meaning and implementation. The witness of one group as to the veracity of its faith claims often sets them at odds with the beliefs of other Christian traditions.

In the nineteenth and twentieth centuries, revivalism and a concern for direct evangelism led many Christian groups to place great emphasis on "witnessing for Christ," a hallmark of Christian discipleship. Clergy and laity alike were instructed in techniques for articulating the "plan of salvation" at every opportunity, calling unconverted individuals to place their faith in Christ. Thus "witnessing" was often thought of primarily as a strategy for personal evangelism aimed at bringing sinners to "a personal experience with Jesus Christ."[2] For many Protestants, from Social Gospel liberals to Holiness Pentecostals, witness was inseparable from the actions of Christians in the world—living a life of holiness grounded in moral rigor of private and public behavior, or challenging the social and spiritual inequities of the age in an effort toward, as Social Gospel advocate Walter Rauschenbusch declared, "Christianizing the social order." The church's witness was evident in the lives of those who chose to follow Christ in ways that modeled the power and presence of the gospel wherever it might take them.[3]

When Mercer University Press contacted me about a volume of collected writings from my experiences in the academy and the church, I

---

[2] Bill J. Leonard, *The Challenge of Being Baptist* (Waco TX: Baylor University Press, 2011) 75–94; William McLoughlin, *Revivals, Awakenings and Reform* (Chicago: University of Chicago Press, 1980).
[3] Walter Rauschenbusch, *Christianizing the Social Order* (Waco TX: Baylor University Press, 2010); and Grant Wacker, *Heaven Below: Early Pentecostals and American Culture* (Cambridge MA: Harvard University Press, 2001).

was honored, recalling an earlier, similar work by my friend and former colleague Walter (Buddy) Shurden, titled *Distinctively Baptist: Essays on Baptist History*. The materials that I have gathered come from various contexts of my life and work. Some are previously unpublished essays on religious issues; some were presented as papers at academic societies or lectureships, while others were written for classroom use with students. Many of the lectures relate to questions of Baptist history and identity with particular concerns for the state of "Baptistness" for the future. As Baptist groups, old and new, confront the organizational, demographic, and theological transitions, issues of identity were bound to arise. If some of the materials overlap a bit, especially those related to Baptists, I apologize, but hope that the context accounts for the need to reassert continuing concepts and heritage.

Other materials are sermons preached in a variety of congregations across the years. Years ago I published a collection of sermons titled *Word of God Across the Ages: Using Church History in Preaching* that focused on specific individuals—St. Francis, Martin Luther, Roger Williams, Sojourner Truth, and Lottie Moon, among them.[4] After that, I realized that the publication of sermons should be done with fear and trembling since they are never written in a vacuum and are addressed to specific congregations in distinctive historical circumstances. In other words, they become dated almost as soon as they are preached. The sermons printed here are offered with similar caution.

Another segment of the book contains addresses that I wrote during my term as dean of the Wake Forest University School of Divinity. From our beginning in 1999 until my term ended in 2010, it was my privilege to give an annual introductory address to the entering class of students and to offer remarks at the graduation ceremony in which the School of Divinity presents degrees to Master of Divinity students after they have been conferred by the university president at the university graduation service. Some of those addresses are provided here in the section titled, "In the Divinity School." They are reflections on the nature of Christian ministry and the role of theological education for church and society.

The final section is a collection of representative columns written twice monthly for the Associated Baptist Press, in a series also titled

---

[4] Bill J. Leonard, *Word of God Across the Ages* (Greenville SC: Smyth & Helwys Publishers, 1991).

"Can I Get a Witness?" They are essentially op-ed responses to a variety of issues, past and present, in American religious and cultural life. The column forced me to confront such topics in ways I had not done so before, addressing contemporary controversies and cultural developments with an eye to their historical roots or implications. I am grateful to Associated Baptist Press for permission to reproduce some of them here.

Many of the essays in this volume address the changing religious environment that impacts every ecclesial community in American religious life. I have long suggested that churches and other religious institutions are living in a time of permanent transition in which old systems of organization and identity are changing, reforming, declining, and even disappearing from the ecclesiastical landscape. Denominations, once the primary means for organizing religious communities in America, are now only one of multiple options and venues for consolidating and coalescing around a specific theology and praxis. Fewer Americans think of their primary religious identity in terms of a denominational identity. The non-denominationalizing of American faith communities illustrates that new reality. Thus, methods for offering Christian witness are undergoing significant reevaluation. In every era, the witness of the church remains a work in progress as congregations celebrate their shared identity through worship, instruction and care for those who are hurting, while refining other ministries in response to location, conscience or a specific historical moment.

In a book titled, *American Grace: How Religion Divides and Unites Us*, published in 2010, professors Robert Putnam (Harvard) and David Campbell (Notre Dame) survey major opinion polls related to religious life in America from the 1970s to the 2000s. At the heart of their large and significant work is their reflection on these current trends:

American evangelicals, the nation's largest religious segment, reached their statistical peak in the 1990s at around 28 percent and are currently plateaued at some 24 percent of the population. Putnam and Campbell consider evangelicals to be related primarily to non-denominational churches, noting that if they had referred only to denominational evangelicals, "Baptists and the like," the "decline of evangelical Protestants would have been sharper."[5]

Roman Catholics, the largest single religious tradition in the US, represent some 20 percent of the population, but the Anglo-Catholic element of that community shows dramatic decline. Attendance at weekly mass has dropped significantly in the last five to eight years.

"Nones," those who claim no religious affiliation or participation, are now the third-largest segment of the population, up from 7 percent a few years ago to around 17 percent in the latest polls.

"Mainline" denominations continue to decline, now representing some 13 percent of the population.[6]

Additional studies by the Pew Forum on Religion and Public Life suggest that the "nones" may represent as much as one fifth of the American population. They perhaps represent one third of the so-called "millennial" generation, ages 18 to 35.[7]

What are some current responses to this phenomenon among Christians?

Some insist that this is the statistical verification of what the church has known for centuries: human nature is fallen and corrupt; sinful human beings will run from grace every chance they get. The new polls reveal that the veneer of religiosity in American has finally broken down and the church should reaffirm its calling as a hospice for sinners.

Others suggest that declines offer further evidence of the corruption of an American society where secularism is normative, traditional values are murky or disappearing, and religion is ignored or ridiculed in the public square. Churches should reassert these moral imperatives (the list often varies among communions) and act prophetically in the culture.

Still others see the rise of the "nones" as a result of the church's failure to sustain its evangelistic task, aggressively declaring the gospel to the lost. Churches should retell the "old, old story" with greater determination, even as they differ on the methods for doing so.

Others claim that many people are leaving religion behind because of the actions and behavior of religious institutions and individuals who:

---

[5] Robert D. Putnam and David E. Campbell, *American Grace: How Religion Divides and Unites Us* (New York: Simon & Schuster, 2010) 105.

[6] Ibid., 134–60.

[7] The Pew Forum on Religion and Public Life (9 October 2012).

a) no longer live up to their traditional religious values, b) engage in myopic religious debates that distract them from pressing social and spiritual disorders, c) treat specific individuals or families in ways that foster hurt and disillusionment, d) are trapped in a survival mode that saps creative and redemptive energy, e) all of these, f) none of the above.

Given those varying diagnoses, might it be time to rethink the idea behind and practice of the term witness? Might religious communions revisit their approach to a society where Christianity, especially the cultural but no longer numerically dominant Protestant community, is fast losing its implicit privilege? As churches choose to do just that, might they ask?

What is our most essential calling, and how do we actualize it in our community?

What does it mean to turn from self-preservation to self-sacrifice as a community of faith?

What are the most pressing needs around us, and how do we address them even if some people choose not to join us in that response?

Does our witness in a given community foster energy for or indifference to the dynamics of the Gospel?

What signature ministries might we develop that encourage our churches to thrive—energize communicants for ministry in specific local, regional, or global ways—before fretting over numerical growth or decline?

If the essays in this volume facilitate a reexamination of the nature of Christian and ecclesial witness in twenty-first-century America, they will have done their duty.

At a breakfast honoring the memory of Martin Luther King, Jr., one of the speakers quoted this statement attributed to the slain civil rights leader and Baptist preacher: "True evil lies not in the depraved act of the one, but in the silence of the many." If Dr. King was correct, then a response to the question "Can I get a witness?" is required of us all.

—Bill J. Leonard
Lent 2013

PART I: ESSAYS AND LECTURES

# Perspectives on Baptist Denominationalism:
## Anticipating the Future

In 1976, in lectures at the Southern Baptist Theological Seminary, historian Martin E. Marty made an observation that turned out to be both fateful and ironic. He noted that in the last quarter of the twentieth century three American religious subgroups had retained a surprising degree of "intactness." These included the Mormons, African-American churches and Southern white Protestants, particularly the Southern Baptist Convention (SBC).[1] Intactness meant that these groups retained a continuity with their past and were able to articulate an identity for their constituency in the present. Marty's comments about the SBC were correct, if only for about fifteen minutes. The words were barely spoken when America's largest Protestant denomination began to come apart. Conflicts between so-called SBC moderates and fundamentalists, which began officially in 1979, continue to dominate denominational affairs. Indeed, after almost two decades of The Controversy, intactness seems the last word one might use to describe America's most publicly and permanently volatile denomination.

How did it happen? There is no end to theories, analyses, and blame inside and outside the convention. Some suggest it simply illustrates the capture of a denomination by its right wing—a phenomenon not unlike earlier left-wing "takeovers" of other major American communions. Others see it as a basic "course correction" undertaken to prevent the SBC from going "the way of the Presbyterians and the Methodists." Still others see it as a painful but intriguing confluence of sociological, political, economic, and theological, forces impacting all denominations but sweeping across the SBC in specific ways. Whatever the explanation, when it comes to the current state of the SBC, several things are abundantly clear, even for those Southern Baptists whose ability for denial is unsurpassed.

---

[1] Martin E. Marty, (lectures, Southern Baptist Theological Seminary, Louisville KY, April 1976); see also, Marty, "The Protestant Experience and Perspective," in Rodger Van Allen, ed., *American Religious Values and the Future of America* (Philadelphia: Fortress Press, 1978) 30–51.

Although the fundamentalists "won" the takeover battle, many of them are fast recognizing that winning has not delivered the anticipated results. Fundamentalists now dominate the national convention and are fast reshaping the SBC in their image. Agendas relative to biblical inerrancy and rightist social concerns dominate their programs. Yet in spite of their success, they have been unable to reestablish a denominational center or recreate a new sense of intactness. Rather, fragmentation has become the order of the day among and within the multiple subgroups that exist inside the SBC.

Moderates "lost," but most remain within the denomination, unable to abandon the SBC and the myth that it imparted to them. Some moderates still hope to retake and restore their beloved denomination, while others continue to wait for the "pendulum to swing back" to the old center (I believe it fell off in 1985 or thereabouts). Still others are refocusing energy on new societies of their own creation represented by the Alliance Baptists and the Cooperative Baptist Fellowship, Smyth & Helwys Publishers, and Baptist Theological Seminary at Richmond, to name only a few. Through it all there remain innumerable Southern Baptists who still claim that nothing has changed or who insist that this is simply a "preachers' fight" like others that periodically afflict the SBC. Even after massive change in denominational agencies, denial is deep and enduring.

Such denial is increasingly difficult to maintain, however. Even a brief survey of current events illustrates the dilemma. In 1991, SBC moderates formed the Cooperative Baptist Fellowship (CBF), a coalition of churches and individuals remaining inside the SBC but redirecting funds and energies toward a variety of "new endeavors." Numerous Southern Baptist universities—Baylor, Furman, Stetson, and Samford—have renegotiated their relationship with their respective state Baptist conventions. The Woman's Missionary Union, Auxiliary to the SBC, has established new program goals that open the door to work with all SBC churches including (potentially at least) those of the CBF. Funda-mentalists now speak of "SBC-sanctioned churches," a euphemism that distinguishes congregations supporting the traditional Cooperative Program of collective giving from those that do not. The fact is, many congregations—fundamentalist and moderate—now give members a variety of options for where they wish their money to go inside and outside the local church.

I have written about the conflict in the SBC for decades, so I am not going to mince words about its implications for understanding American denominationalism.[2] My thesis revolves around the following observations:

First, the denominational center of the SBC was forged in the cultural ethos of the American South and the defeat in the Civil War, as well as through participation in the "religion of the Lost Cause," and the prevailing racism of the region.

Second, the establishment of a denominational center protected the constituency from the dominance of numerous theological, regional, and popular subgroups that, implicitly or explicitly, sought to impose their sectarian agendas on the entire convention.

Third, over a period of time the center shaped, and was shaped by, a denominational identity that created a programmatic mechanism for defining the convention and its cooperating churches.

Fourth, that programmatic center served as a kind of regulator, a safety valve that kept the Southern Baptist penchant for incessant controversy from evolving into full-blown schism.

Fifth, the center was built on, and maintained by, programmatic and statistical success. The success of denominational programs was evidence that the sacrifices necessary for its maintenance, whether financial or ideological, were worth the price.

Sixth, the centrist theology of the denomination was specific enough to be identifiably Baptist but general enough to allow for considerable regional and doctrinal diversity. At times it was rhetorically orthodox and popularly heretical on the left and the right. While Baptists seemed consumed with maintaining theological correctness, and talked as if they were paragons of orthodoxy, their popular theology sometimes led them into heresy on such issues as justification, sanctification, and ecclesiology.

Seventh, the denominational center took many of its cues from the prevailing culture on such matters as race, corporate organization, and church/state relations.

Eighth, the centrist coalition was so obsessed with avoiding schism and retaining numerical strength that it sowed the seeds of its own

---

[2] Bill J. Leonard, *God's Last and Only Hope: The Fragmentation of the SBC* (Grand Rapids: Eerdmans, 1990).

demise. By retaining incompatible subgroups, the ultimate destruction of the old center was ensured.

Ninth, the once-impregnable center collapsed in the latter quarter of the twentieth century. While something called the Southern Baptist Convention continues to exist, it is merely a shell for an ever-fragmenting assortment of subgroups, each as yet incapable of reestablishing a new center for the denomination or for itself.

Tenth, the collapse of the denominational mechanism of the SBC has created a vacuum in terms of education, mission, evangelism, and organization throughout churches and state conventions long related to the huge denomination. Whatever else Baptists may discuss regarding denominationalism, they must address the question of identity.

Now, there should be something in all that to offend everybody. Let me elaborate on what I have suggested. Time and space do not allow me to address every one of those issues in detail. My primary concern is with the question of the denominational center, how it came and how it went.

As Sidney Mead and others have written, denominationalism created a center or centers around which American religious groups could unite. It became the "shape" of Protestantism in America. With the constitutional protection of religious liberty and the demise of religious establishments, the denomination became a way of organizing religious institutions in the new nation. For two centuries, denominations helped religious organizations shape a center, create an identity, and form a mythology around which a diverse regional, theological, and popular constituency could cooperate. The center did not eliminate diversity and conflict—far from it—but created an environment in which numerous factions could join together in common endeavor for missions, publications, evangelism, and educational endeavors.[3] Indeed, American religious life tended to "denominationalize" groups as diverse as Baptists, Mormons, Roman Catholics, and Jews.

On the threshold of the twentieth century, religious groups in America are experiencing a significant transition in organizational structure and identity. While denominations continue to exercise influence, they are increasingly one option for a variety of religious affiliations and connections. That reality leads me to suggest ten

---

[3] Sidney Mead, *The Lively Experiment* (New York: Harper & Row, 1963) 108.

observations relative to the future of religious life in the new millennium, each of which is related to the question of CBF as a denomination for the future. Those who wish to denominationalize the Cooperative Baptist Fellowship should give serious attention to the following realities.

First, it is clear that fewer religious Americans think of their primary religious identity in terms of a denominational identity. Denominational loyalty is now much less important to religious Americans than it was in the past. One Alabama Baptist leader comments that this generation of church members is much less committed to "brand-name" than to the particular ethos of local communities of faith. Thus, when Baptists talk of establishing a new denomination apart from the Cooperative Baptist Fellowship or some other entity, one is compelled to ask why they feel the need. Indeed, the latter days of the twentieth century have been the worst time to take over an old denomination or to start a new one. In light of these changing realities, might we look for new ways of understanding the nature of religious cooperation and communicating Christian, indeed Baptist, identity?

Second, regional and local identities are stronger than national affiliations. Episcopalians, Presbyterians, Baptists, and Pentecostals are downsizing their national organizations in light of changing loyalties and declining revenues.

Third, local congregations are developing multiple alliances and connections inside and outside denominations. For example, many congregations once utilized educational literature from their specific denomination. Recent trends indicate that many of these churches are now "shopping around" for materials from a variety of sources. Desktop publishing offers opportunities for some churches or cooperating groups to carry out their own publishing on specific issues and concerns aimed at particular target groups.

Fourth, local congregations and individual Christians are discovering multiple methods and opportunities for facilitating the missionary imperative of the church. Short-term mission activities that involve members in direct missionary endeavors are captivating congregations across the theological spectrum. Likewise, churches are increasingly open to participating in multiple missionary programs—local, regional, and national—with denominational and non-denominational groups.

Fifth, Baptist students are responding to multiple options for theological education. Growing numbers of students are choosing to secure ministerial training at schools inside and outside the Baptist fold. While some continue to attend one of the six SBC seminaries, others now select one of the new Baptist-related institutions founded during the 1990s. Still others look to non-Baptist schools. Churches must learn new ways of recruiting potential ministers from a variety of graduate schools. Denominationalizing efforts on the part of CBF may make it more difficult to coordinate relationships with students and schools.

Sixth, most Baptist congregations remain pluralistic communities of faith with persons spread across the theological and institutional spectrum, a response to the changing times. The genius of the Southern Baptist Convention was its ability to transmit identity and loyalty to a particular tradition. Many people affiliated with SBC-related churches but opposed to the current fundamentalist control still cannot bring themselves to break with the denomination of their forbearers. Younger constituents do not have similar loyalties to the SBC, nor are they ready to identify with a new Baptist entity. Creating a new denomination may force persons to make decisions for participation in a new institution that they are unable or unwilling to make for a variety of reasons.

Seventh, after years of controversy in the SBC, many Baptists simply mistrust denominations all together and are hesitant to involve themselves in a new endeavor that may create the same hierarchy or bureaucracy that characterized the SBC. In fact, suspicion of denominations is evident throughout the Baptist constituency. Individuals and local churches may be more willing to identify with subgroups loosely related to the CBF—Women in Ministry, Baptist Joint Committee, theological schools, mission endeavors—rather than a denomination which requires allegiance to multiple entities.

Eighth, Baptist organizations are in such a state of transition that denominationalizing may serve to limit CBF rather than extend its influence and cooperation to numerous bodies and groups. For example, it is not yet clear what forms the Baptist state conventions will take as they reorganize themselves in response to changing times. The actions of the Baptist General Convention of Texas in redefining their financial ties to the national SBC in 1995 can be seen as a form of denominationalizing on the part of one powerful regional organization. One could make the case that those efforts mark the beginning of what could become the sixth-largest denomination in the United States! If CBF chooses to declare itself a denomination, it could narrow its constituency considerably rather than becoming a clearinghouse for multiple Baptist groups in need of multiple relationships.

Ninth, perhaps the most effective response to these transitions would be to develop a form of the traditional society method that served Baptists well in an earlier era. When Baptists mistrusted hierarchies and were uncertain as to how to cooperate, when they were willing to unite through specific subgroups (societies) for missions, publication, evangelism, and education, they found the society method extremely helpful. The society articulated a Baptist identity, united groups of Baptists in significant endeavors, and still allowed for freedom of participation and support for specific causes and activities.

Tenth, perhaps the real problem for the Baptist denominational future involves the issue of identity. The denominational mechanisms that facilitated identity and enabled traditions to be passed on to succeeding generations are fast breaking apart or addressing only one of the multiple subgroups that still compose the SBC. Perhaps the most essential question is: When all is said and done, what will remain which is discernably, historically Baptist? We might also ask: How will Baptists, whatever their affiliation, pass on an identifiably Baptist tradition to their children? Will a kind of generic theological or political correctness, left and right, replace a sense of Baptistness, whatever that may be? How will local autonomy be sustained? What theology of baptism and the Lord's Supper will be passed on to a new generation? What mechanism for calling persons to ministry can be maintained? In short, will all these subgroups give their constituencies a place to stand that is, or should be, discernably and affirmatively Baptist? CBF could address those issues in ways that would facilitate dialogue among multiple groups now taking shape in Baptist life.

In conclusion, therefore, I would urge participants in the Cooperative Baptist Fellowship to continue, and indeed sharpen, its position as a clearinghouse for multiple Baptist groups inside and outside the old SBC. This would permit churches to allow freedom of choice among their members as to which Baptist group they choose to support. It would allow existing subgroups—theological schools, publication companies, state conventions, specialized societies—to relate to the CBF and thus to each other, gathering at its annual meetings and contributing to the diversity of its constituents. It would also create the possibility for common endeavors and relationships with Baptist and non-Baptist organizations, specifically American Baptist Churches/USA and various National Baptist groups. It would also permit CBF to offer significant insight into the nature of Baptist identity for the future. Through a society approach, the CBF could facilitate new ways of networking for organizations and individuals alike. To form a denominational structure now may limit the mission and ministry of an organization that has great potential to renew and reshape Baptist life in a new millennium.

# An Audacious Identity[1]

In 1646, Anglican preacher Daniel Featley wrote of the "Dippers" rampant in England:

> They preach, and print, and practice their heretical impieties openly; they hold their conventicles weekly in our chief Cities, and Suburbs thereof, and there prophesy by turns; and...they build one another in the faith of their sect, to the ruin of their souls; they flock in great multitudes to their Jordans, and both sexes enter into the River, and are dipt after their manner with a kind of spell containing...their erroneous tenets....And as they defile our Rivers with their impure washings, and our pulpits with their false prophecies and fanatical enthusiasms, so the presses sweat and grown under the load of their blasphemies.[2]

For some people then and now, Baptists will never be more than a bunch of fanatical, soul-ruining, river-defiling dippers. Let's ask this tonight, "every head bowed, every eye closed, no one looking around." How many of you have ever felt at least a little embarrassed to call yourself a Baptist? Raise your hands. To those who lifted your hands, thank you for your honesty. The rest of you are lying!

Now get over it. Like the earliest Christians, Baptists had an audacious identity from the start. Tonight's scripture text, written in the early second century, audaciously declares of those who identified with the "Jesus Way:" "We are the children of God." Then adds abruptly: "but the world does not recognize us." (1 John 3:1) And why should it? Salvation through a crucified, underclass, Palestinian Jew who's only recorded writing was in the dirt?—Children of God, indeed! The church grew, but the critics remained. The third-century Roman philosopher Celsus assessed the Christians of his day accordingly:

> The following are the rules laid down by them: Let no one come to us who has been instructed or who is wise or prudent (for such are deemed

---

[1] This lecture was delivered at the Annual Meeting of the Cooperative Baptist Fellowship, Charlotte NC, 24 June 2010.

[2] Daniel Featley, *The Dippers Dipt, or, the Anabaptists Duck'd and Plung'd over head and Eares, at a Disputation at Southwark* (London: Nicholas Bourne and Richard Royston, 1646) n.p.

evil by us), but if there be any ignorant or unintelligent or uninstructed or foolish persons, let them come with confidence. By which words (acknowledging that such persons are worthy [children] of their God) they are able to gain only the silly, the mean, and the stupid, with women and children.[3]

Contemporary critic Christopher Hitchens echoes Celsus in his recent assertion that the Protestant reformer John Calvin "may seem like a far-off figure to us, but those who used to grab and use power in his name are still among us and go by the softer names of Presbyterians and Baptists."[4] Faith-tinged identities consume and corrupt, empower and embarrass all at once, don't they? For many persons inside and outside the church Christians in general, and Baptists in particular, often look less like "children of God," than childishly "silly, mean, and stupid." And we sometimes act the part, don't we?

Which brings us back to the early Baptists: They are not models to which we should return, but spiritual guides who illustrate ways to understand ourselves and our witness in the world. English Puritans in exile, huddled in a "bakeshop" in Amsterdam, they constituted their new community around believers' baptism in 1609. Two years later, on their way back home, they united around these haunting words:

> That the church of Christ is a company of faithful people separated from the world by the word & spirit of God, being knit unto the Lord, & one another, by Baptism upon their own confession of the faith and sins.[5]

Shall I repeat it so you can take it all in?

In that single sentence those exiles, not yet practicing immersion, not yet named Baptists, said what it meant to be children of God. At our best, four hundred years later, that is still who we are.

They began with an audacious faith. Membership in the church, they said, is grounded in an experience of grace, not geography. Baptism should be administered on the basis of one's own "confession of faith and sins," not enforced by the state-based or culture-privileged religious establishment of a so-called Christian nation. Do you understand how

---

[3] Origen, *Contra Celsus* (*Against Celsus*), in *The Ante-Nicene Fathers.* See www.blufton.edu/-humanities/1/celsus.htm.

[4] Christopher Hitchens, *God Is Not Great* (New York: Twelve, 2007), 233–34.

[5] William L. Lumpkin, *Baptist Confessions of Faith* (Valley Forge: Judson Press, 1974) 119.

radical that idea was in seventeenth-century Europe where citizenship and church membership were linked inseparably? These Baptists gazed at their world and saw what many of their contemporaries overlooked: A Believers' Church where no one could claim membership save those who could profess faith for themselves, uncoerced by state or religious establishments. This understanding of faith set Baptists at odds with both the church and the culture of their day. In many places it still does.

How might their audacious identity impact us? First, we welcome everyone who comes to us, whatever their faith or lack thereof, but we ask all who would claim membership to profess their faith in Jesus Christ. With those early Baptists we too must make our "own confession of faith and sins." You can't confess your faith, if you won't confess your sins. Contrary to popular preaching in our religious culture, grace is not an entitlement; it is a gift by which we cast ourselves on Christ and acknowledge our brokenness in the sure belief that the Kingdom of God is indeed within our reach.

Second, we cannot take for granted that people in postmodern America, even those who show up at church, have the slightest idea of what we are talking about. So we have to keep retelling the "old, old story," explaining through traditions old and new why we think faith and baptism are wonderfully important in a human life. And if we are going to take the responsibility of baptizing children, then we have to take the responsibility of "confirming" their faith when the hard moral dilemmas—when their sins—find them out in adolescence and beyond. Baptism is not the end of the journey it is the beginning. Let's reaffirm that together.

Third, let's be less concerned for a single plan of salvation that completes a required transaction than for a lifelong process of conversion that transforms human beings day by day. On a trip with students to Bucharest, Romania, I was privileged to be present when Dr. Oti Bunaciu, pastor of the Providence Baptist church there, baptized a group of Roma/Gypsy men and women in a baptistery that soars above the pulpit. As they entered the water, Dr. Bunaciu inquired of each candidate: "Are you willing to be a follower of Jesus Christ?" When he asked a young Roma woman, probably sixteen or seventeen, she blurted out with tears: "Oh yes, every day for the rest of my life." Faith in Christ is our common confession, day by day, even if the process varies.

Some of us got saved hard, sweating our way to salvation as if we'd been to hell one afternoon and had come back to tell about it; others were guided by spiritual mentors who nurtured Jesus into us along the way; still others broke through to grace after incessant struggles with life's outer or inner horrors, and others of us don't know exactly how Jesus ever found us, we just know he did.

And that audacious faith demands an audacious witness. Nineteenth-century British historian Edward Underhill, insisted that "a distinguishing…trait" of the early Baptists was their claim, "for the church and for the conscience, of freedom from all human control." He wrote that the Baptist insistence that "faith is the gift of God" "brought them into collision with every form of human invention in the worship of God." "For this," Underhill suggested, "the Baptists bore cheerfully, *cruel mocking, and scourging; yea, moreover bonds and imprisonments,* and death."[6]

The demand for religious liberty and its resulting religious pluralism was perhaps Baptists' first great witness in the world. They force us to ask: Can we give a witness? What compels our individual or collective consciences here and now? Christian witness lies at the heart of who we are, how we act, and what we do when the times get out of hand.

A church without a witness is a church without an identity whatever name it may call itself. Worship is witness sure enough. Worship links "ordinary time" and "sacred time" day to day, week to week. Baptism and the Lord's Supper are witness, the word of God without words, enacting the promise of God's presence in our midst. Feeding the hungry, clothing the naked, binding up the broken, and calling persons to faith is at the heart of the church's continuing witness, beyond a doubt. But where does witness and conscience intersect or collide? In the past, in the South, we white Baptists sinned against our consciences, trashed our witness with our support of slavery and Jim Crow. What piece of the Gospel are we trashing now? Beyond worship wars, culture wars, and church-growth strategies, what is our witness to the highest mandates and deepest passions of the Jesus Way?

Two congregations illustrate such witness for me these days. For the past five years, Highland Baptist Church in Louisville, Kentucky—a predominately Caucasian congregation—has responded to drive-by

[6] Edward Bean Underhill, Introduction, *The Records of a Church of Christ, meeting in Broadmead, Bristol, 1640–1687* (London: J. Haddon, 1847) xliv.

shootings in their city through an alliance with Afric
churches that sends clergy and laity to the murder sites for
vigils and then plants crosses in their churchyards with the ........
victims. Will those actions help stop the shootings? They hope so, but
even if murders continue, a witness has been given by churches, both
black and white, compelled by conscience to confront the madness. What
a witness!

Four years ago, some folks from Wilshire Baptist Church, Dallas,
decided to ordain Andrew Daugherty and send him out to Rock Wall,
Texas, to plant a new congregation called Christchurch, as a witness for
those who are outside of, or washed out of, traditional Texas churches.
They had a good run in two successive public gathering places, touching
the lives of a variety of persons who discovered, rediscovered, or jump-
started their faith. Next Sunday, Christchurch, Baptist, will end its
ministry with a consensus that they have run their course, lived out the
fullness of the Gospel in one community as best they could. Was that
fledgling church a failure? No, it was a witness, reminding us of what
the early Baptists surely knew: Not every calling has to last forever.
When we start or finish something for Jesus, we have to follow our
consciences at the beginning and the end. Thank God.

Don't start with the question of whether your church is thriving or
declining, growing or dying. Begin by asking whether you have a
witness in the world, a call to conscience that is worth pursuing whether
the initial endeavor lives or dies. William Sloan Coffin was right, let's
risk something big for something good, wherever it takes us.

We are, after all, an audacious community, we Baptists, with a
checkered past and an uncertain future, "knit together," as our
forbearers said. People never really joined us easily, it seems.

These days I think often about Ann Hasseltine, who as a student at
New England's Branford Academy in the early 1800s read Jonathan
Edwards's monumental work *The History of the Work of Redemption* and
decided she had to be a missionary. But she was a woman and churches
weren't sending out women on global endeavors, so she looked around
for a husband who would help her get there. She found Adoniram
Judson, a recent graduate of Williams College. They married in 1812 and
immediately set out for India as Congregational missionaries. On the
boat they studied the Greek New Testament together and became
Baptists, an act so scandalous that Ann hurriedly wrote to a

Congregational friend, "Can you, my dear Nancy, still love me, still desire to hear from me, when I tell you I have become a Baptist?" Of their method, she said: "We procured the best authors on both sides, compared them with the Scriptures, examined and reexamined the sentiments of Baptists and Pedobaptists, and were finally compelled from a conviction of truth, to embrace the former. Thus, my dear Nancy, we are confirmed Baptists, not because we wished to be, but because truth compelled us to be. We have endeavored to count the cost, and be prepared for the many severe trials resulting from this change of sentiment."[7]

And was there a cost. The Judsons went to Burma and began a new mission there, ever in need of funds, friends, and protection from hostile governments. Adoniram Judson was arrested and imprisoned; Ann bribed the guards to get him food and medicine. He was released; she died in childbirth in 1826 at the age of 37. Five years ago this summer I had dinner at the Baptist World Congress with the president of the Baptist Union of Burma/Myanmar who described himself as the spiritual great-great-great-grandson of the Judsons. Not all of Ann's children were stillborn.

If conscience dictates I suppose we can rip the word Baptist out of our literature, paint over it on our church signs, or delete it from the our Web page, Facebook, Twitter, and podcasts. But before we do, let's admit that there is no generic Christianity divorced from a community or an identity that centers us in the world or the Kingdom of God. As Baptists, we are knit together with the Amsterdam exiles, the Gypsy teenager in the Bucharest baptistery, and the black and white Baptists who pray together in the killing fields of Louisville; we are knit together with an audacious young missionary compelled by conscience to become a Baptist even when she didn't want to, a gangly teenager who will stay behind, and with a congregation in Rock Wall, Texas, as they sing their last hymn together this Sunday morning. We are all knit into that "body of broken bones," as Thomas Merton called the church.[8]

---

[7] H. Leon McBeth, *Sourcebook for Baptist Heritage* (Nashville: Broadman Press, 1990, 201–08.

[8] Thomas P. McDonnell, ed., *A Thomas Merton Reader* (Garden City NY: Image Books, 1974) 320.

St. Paul said it best when he wrote to the Corinthians; a church we know was Baptist because they were obsessed with preaching, food, and sex:

> We recommend ourselves by the innocence of our behavior, our grasp of truth, our patience and kindliness; by gifts of the Holy Spirit, by sincere love, by declaring the truth, by the power of God. We wield the weapons of righteousness in right hand and left. Honor and dishonor, praise and blame, are alike our lot: we are the impostors who speak the truth, the unknown ones whom everyone knows; dying we still live on; disciplined by suffering, we are not done to death; in our sorrows we have always cause for joy; poor ourselves, we bring wealth to many; penniless, we own the world. (2 Cor. 6:4–10, NEB)

Let's stop worrying about our name and start reclaiming our witness; let's quit fretting over the loss of culture dominance and turn loose our consciences. Let's go out as children of God, born again, and again, and again in one of the church's clearly dysfunctional, but grace-filled families; children of God in the Water and at the Table, in the Word and in the world, children of God, KNIT together, knit together, knit together—by grace. Amen.

# Hologram Preaching and Disposable Communion: Un-Real Presence in a New Millennium[1]

In the fall of 1995, two reports appeared in the secular media that provided further evidence of the changing face of religion in contemporary America. At first glance, the reports seemed almost inconsequential. One was disclosed in a story of yet another mega-church extending its influence throughout yet another metropolitan area; the other was announced in a simple press release from a major denomination. Taken together, however, they provided insights into certain practical and theological challenges facing American religious communities on the way to the next millennium. The reports detailed two new methods—hologram preaching and disposable communion sets—which churches may use to communicate the Christian religion in a changing world. Some view these methods as simply pragmatic, even avant-garde, means for accomplishing certain spiritual ends. Others suggest that they are theologically and liturgically detrimental to the church's basic identity. Even if they do not become enduring traditions, hologram preaching and disposable communion sets demonstrate something of the opportunities and temptations that confront the modern (or postmodern) church.

The technology for, and possible use of, hologram preaching was made public on National Public Radio's show *All Things Considered* in an intriguing profile of Second Baptist Church, Houston, Texas, one of America's best-known mega-congregations. Churches like Second Baptist are the focus of frequent media attention and are often viewed as fostering significant new "trends" in American ecclesiastical life. With the millennium at hand and most traditional religious institutions in transition, if not downright decline, some media analysts wonder if the mega-church is the church of the future.

A mega-church may be defined as a congregation—urban and/or suburban—of several thousand members led by a charismatic-authority-

---

[1] This paper was presented at the fall meeting of the American Academy of Religion in 1999.

figure-CEO founder/pastor, providing specialty services for target constituencies and organized around distinct marketing techniques. Its leaders, most of whom represent segments of the evangelical wing of American Christianity, insist that they retain conservative theology and ethics while "packaging" their message in a language and media that an essentially "unchurched" generation can understand. Indeed, many such churches consider themselves "seeker oriented," aiming at persons who have little background in traditional religion or who long ago wrote off religious institutions as irrelevant or insensitive to their situation. Mega-church promoters suggest that most churches are not user-friendly to the unchurched who are uncomfortable with the formal liturgies or "corpse-cold" "sanctuaries" of most church buildings. Most secularized Americans are uncomfortable in church because they do not know the hymns, appreciate the symbols, or want to take time to learn proper liturgical procedures necessary for participation in most services. Services in many mega-churches are often geared to "seekers," and characterized by informal, folksy style, upbeat music including informal praise choruses displayed on screens overhead, the use of drama, and sermons addressing practical issues of everyday living. Congregations are large—mammoth, even— but a sense of community is best discovered in innumerable small group experiences built around Bible study classes, prayer groups, exercise programs, or other service projects.

A staff of specialized ministers serves specific subgroups in the congregation. Many are started "from scratch," and grown from the beginning according to intentional marketing styles. Buildings are constructed more like shopping malls than cathedrals, with a multipurpose, state-of-the-art "worship center." Often there are food courts, fitness facilities, and enclosed, park-like areas with trees and fountains. Proponents of this ecclesiastical approach insist that they are simply mirroring the medieval cathedral, providing a church as a spiritual and cultural center of specific communities, becoming a multipurpose institution in sync with fast-paced and ever-changing social and familial trends. In fact, many such congregations devote significant time to long-range planning in anticipation of trends five to twenty-five years hence, constantly seeking to stay on the cusp of social agendas. While Willow Creek Community Church outside Chicago is perhaps the nation's best known, most imitated, and most studied mega-church, Second Baptist, Houston, is not far behind.

Whatever else it may be, Second Baptist is a trendsetter, charting new paths for communicating the Gospel's "old, old story" in a new age. In fact, Second Baptist seems mega in almost every detail. The church now claims more than twenty thousand members and projects continued growth well into the next century. On Sundays, multiple services are conducted morning and evening in a "worship center" that seats more than five thousand people. The "church plant" includes a bowling alley and a full-service physical fitness center operating throughout the week. A huge ministerial staff maintains specialized programs for age groups ranging from infants to senior adults. When interviewed for NPR, the ministers unashamedly acknowledged that elaborate marketing techniques readily inform their organizational efforts to "reach people for Christ." Indeed, the *All Things Considered* report highlighted the church's study of Disney World as a model for attracting people, engaging their energies, and even moving them from their cars to the church facilities. (Vast parking lots are divided into sections identified with biblical names.) Every effort is made to anticipate cultural trends and stay ahead of the game in responding to the spiritual and demographic needs of the church in the world as it is and as it shall be in the new millennium. This attempt to envision the future has led the church to purchase land for a new "campus" in suburban Houston, an area where population growth is assured and where large numbers of "unchurched" persons already reside.

At the center of the Second Baptist enterprise is the Rev. Edwin Young, the church's senior pastor, spiritual leader, and chief executive officer. Young, former president of the Southern Baptist Convention and charismatic shepherd of the church, preaches in multiple Sunday worship services that are televised throughout the US in a syndicated program called the *Fellowship of Excitement*. His energetic sermons link Scripture and contemporary life, offering practical responses to issues of family, job, community, and Christian commitment. During the NPR interview, Young insisted that the modern methods utilized so successfully at Second Baptist did not change the traditional message of the gospel but simply refashioned its packaging. He also noted that when the church's new suburban campus was established he would be able to proclaim the Word of God simultaneously to both of Second Baptist's congregations by means of "hologram preaching."

As the leadership of Second Baptist sees it, hologram preaching is simply an effective technological vehicle for offering the message and the messenger to another generation of sinner/consumers. When the plans for organizing a second congregation were originally initiated, it was suggested that pastor Young would be transported between the two churches by helicopter, preaching in both locations as Second Baptist's senior minister and central figure. The technology of hologram preaching, however, now makes it possible for him to be in two places at once, but without the old-fashioned, impersonal television monitor. By means of a hologram, Young's image would be projected in three dimensions, as if he were really present at the same moment in each community of faith.

Such hologram rhetoric is not new to most Americans, at least not to those familiar with popular cinema. Movie-going Americans may recall a scene from the first of the *Star Wars* films when Princess Leah's holographic image is reproduced by the eccentric little droid R2D2. Through a hologram she implores the holy man Obi Wan Kenobi to aid her in the rebellion against the evil Empire. In a lesser-known science-fiction film entitled *THX-1138*—George Lucas's first film, produced in 1971— a white-robed character tells actor Robert Duvall: "I'm a hologram. I'm not real. I've always wanted to be real." At Second Baptist, what once seemed futuristic fantasy could become ecclesiastical verity.

Clearly, Second Baptist Church is anticipating the technological future, applying its advanced methods to ancient homiletic arts. Yet the assertion that such modern techniques have no discernable impact on the "unchanging gospel" is open to question. The theological implications of such activities should not be underestimated.

The NPR report on Second Baptist came at about the same time that the Sunday School Board of the Southern Baptist Convention (Broadman/Holman Publishers) announced that it had become the sole distributor of a new product for use in the celebration of the Lord's Supper. The product is a disposable communion kit composed of a small plastic vial of grape juice topped with an unleavened wafer, both sealed for convenience and sanitary protection.

Marketed under the product name "Remembrance," the disposable communion sets come in boxed six-packs, each of which contains a small brochure describing the merchandise and explaining its proper use. A step-by-step procedure for lifting the proper tab at the proper time is detailed in a series of photographs contained in the brochure. The booklet declares that "Remembrance" communion sets offer "the pure, simple solution...a new alternative to communion...combining both communion wafer and juice in a single, two-part container with a patented double seal." "Remembrance offers unprecedented versatility and efficiency in communion preparation with literally no clean up or waste.... Note the traditional design. The secure, yet easy-opening double seal. Remembrance combines the best modern packaging technology with the timeless traditions of the church."[2] And again, "After many years of research and development with churches, manufacturers and suppliers around the world, it is with great reverence that the Remembrance wafers and juice sets are now available to you. It represents a convenient, hygienic communion alternative made with the highest quality products available, at an affordable price."[3]

What is the church to make of these new liturgical procedures? On one hand, hologram preaching and disposable communion kits may seem no different than the camp meeting and revival techniques used by Methodist circuit riders and Baptist farmer-preachers to bring the Good News to the American frontier. They are simply a set of twenty-first century "New Measures" not unlike those instigated by evangelist Charles G. Finney and other nineteenth-century evangelicals for the purpose of applying the gospel to a new era. Finney's "anxious bench" invited seekers to "come forward" to mourn their sins and invoke the prayers of the faithful in their behalf. He permitted women to pray and testify in "promiscuous" gatherings of both sexes—a scandalous challenge to the prevailing church order. Camp meeting hymns were "peoples' hymns" which replaced or at least rivaled the arcane lined out singing of the psalms. Outdoor revival meetings were organized to attract both the saint and the sinner in a frontier culture where the old ecclesiastical distinctions and institutions did not hold.

Pastor Young's use of hologram preaching, for example, may seem no more ecclesiastically outrageous than John Wesley's decision to begin "field preaching" in eighteenth-century England, stepping outside the church buildings to address the masses directly. Hologram preaching might be as beneficial—even inevitable—for preachers in the twenty-first

---

[2] "Remembrance" accompanying booklet.
[3] Ibid.

century as the microphone was for those in the twentieth century. Logistically, it permits the preacher to have a three-dimensional presence in multiple congregations simultaneously.

Such an epiphany does have a certain biblical élan to it. In describing an appearance of the post-resurrection Christ, John's gospel states: "On the evening of that day, the first day of the week, the doors being shut where the disciples were, for fear of the Jews, Jesus came and stood among them...." (John 20:19 RSV) Through hologram preaching, contemporary homileticians may now be able to anticipate such a phenomenon.

Whether such methods will leave the message unaffected is another matter, however. Indeed, in surprising ways, these two technological developments recall questions of body and spirit, physical and spiritual, long present in the church. In a sense, the preacher as holographic image suggests a kind of twenty-first century Docetism. In the early Christian centuries, Docetism was the belief that Jesus himself only appeared to be human since a perfect and transcendent God could never inhabit a sinful human body. Thus Jesus only seemed to suffer and die on the cross. His post-resurrection appearances were evidence of the ethereal body that had been his all along. Docetism was at least one factor addressed by the Johannine writer's observation "It was there from the beginning; we have heard it; we have seen it with our own eyes; we looked upon it and felt it with our own hands; our theme is the Word which gives life. This word was made visible; we have seen it...(1 John 1:1–2) Does hologram preaching create the possibility for a kind of ministerial Docetism, the pastor who only "seems" to be present with the people, but whose humanity is illusory? Could congregants echo the movie character: "Our minister is a hologram. He is not real." Questions of incarnation surely come to mind. If nothing else the practice could give a whole new meaning to the traditional evangelical, revivalist invitation for seekers to "come forward and shake the preacher's hand" at the end of the service.

Concerning disposable communion kits, it is important to recall that the church has always found ways to revise sacramental practices to meet practical realities. The *Didache*, or *Teaching of the Twelve Apostles*, dating from the early second century, indicates that churches were willing to modify baptismal methods to fit the logistical requirements of the times, specifically the lack of water. It suggests: "Concerning baptism, baptize in this way. Having first rehearsed all these things, baptize in the name of the Father and of the Son and of the Holy Ghost, in living water. But if you have not living water, baptize into other water; and, if thou canst not in cold, in warm. If you have neither, pour water thrice on the head in the name, etc...."[4]

Thus, while maintaining a sacramental norm, the early Christians permitted modifications in the baptismal mode when the situation required more or less water. Likewise, the priest in elaborate vestments consecrating bread and wine in gold vessels in the opulence of a medieval cathedral seems a long way from the simple meal that Jesus shared with friends in the upper room. No doubt one of the major reasons for withholding the cup from the medieval laity was the logistical complexity of dispensing a common cup to thousands gathered for mass. Centuries later, support for the temperance movement led many Protestant groups to change from using fermented wine to grape juice in the Supper. Sanitary concerns and logistical convenience influenced the shift from a common cup to individual communion cups in many congregations. Throwaway communion sets are simply the logical result of temperance sentiment and hygienic efficiency. Are they but the ultimate result of a Protestant theology and practice that "memorialized" Jesus out of the bread and the cup at communion?

Yet, how far can rites and rituals be re-formed before they lose or at least modify theology irreconcilably? How does a pull-tab communion wafer inform the meaning of St. Paul's words: "The bread which we break, is it not participation in the body of Christ? Because there is one bread, we who are many are one body, for we all partake of the one bread." (1 Cor. 10:16–17) Do individualized communion package subtly undermine the idea of the church as the one people of God, a community of sinners bound to Christ and to each other? Can the Eucharist become so sanitized as to lose its powerful sacramental/symbolic meaning as an act of faith and a means of grace?

In short, hologram preaching and disposable communion may indeed challenge one of Christianity's most enduring ideals: the real presence of the Spirit within the community of faith. In its formal sense, the doctrine of the real presence as applied to the Eucharist involves the belief that Christ is physically and spiritually present in and through the bread and the cup. This idea, long present in Roman Catholic, Orthodox,

---

[4] Henry Bettenson, *Documents of the Christian Church* (New York: Oxford University Press, 1963) 90.

and Lutheran theologies of the Lord's Supper, is a valuable motif for understanding many facets of Christian faith.

A rereading of Thomas Aquinas on the doctrine of transubstantiation sounds strangely appropriate for examining the theological and historical implications of our two contemporary events. Concerning transformations in accident and substance in the Supper, St. Thomas wrote:

> Now a thing cannot be in a place where it was not before except either by change of position, or by the conversion of some other thing into it....But it is clear that the body of Christ does not begin to be in the sacrament through change of position....Therefore it remains that the body of Christ can only come to be in the sacrament by means of the conversion of the substance of bread into his body...[5] ...I reply that this conversion is not like natural conversions but is wholly supernatural, effected solely by the power of God....And this is done in this sacrament by the power of God, for the whole substance of bread is converted into the whole substance of Christ's body....Hence this conversion is properly called transub-stantiation.[6]

Again, even Aquinas struggled with the question of body and space, writing, "Now anybody has a position in space according to the mode of spacial dimension, inasmuch as its extension is measured thereby. Hence Christ's body is not in this sacrament as in a place, but in the mode of substance, i.e. in the way in which a substance is confined by dimensions; for the substance of Christ's body takes the place of the substance of bread."[7] Somehow, and I am not sure precisely how, Aquinas's words relate to the theological question of holograms as well as to the real presence of Christ in the Eucharist. Is it possible that contemporary evangelical Protestants are creating mechanisms for a transubstantiation of the preacher while denying such real presence in the Lord's Supper?

Christ's real or at least spiritual presence was a continuing emphasis of many of the reformers and their early heirs. Lutheran and Reformed traditions alike affirmed, in various ways, the uniqueness of the Eucharist and Christ's presence in, with, or alongside the elements. In the Second London Confession of 1677, British Calvinistic Baptists

---

[5] *Summa Theologica,* iiii, Q.lxxv.

[6] Ibid., Article IV.

[7] Ibid., Article VI.

denied transubstantiation, while, like the Westminster Confession of the 1640s, affirming the spiritual presence of Christ in the Eucharist. The document reads:

> The outward Elements in this Ordinance, duly set apart to the uses ordained by Christ, have such relation to him crucified, as that truely, although in terms used figuratively, they are sometimes called by the name of the things they represent, to wit body and Blood of Christ; albeit to substance, and nature, they still remain truly, and only Bread, and Wine, as they were before.[8]

The confession also acknowledges:

> Worthy receivers, outwardly partaking of the visible Elements in this Ordinance, do then also inwardly by faith, really and indeed, yet not carnally, and corporally, but spiritually receive, and feed upon Christ crucified, & all the benefits of his death: the Body and Blood of Christ, being then not corporally, or carnally, but spiritually present to the faith of Believers, in that Ordinance, as the Elements themselves are to their outward senses.[9]

Hologram preaching can deny the real presence of the pastor among the people of God. It literally creates an image of the church's minister, present but not present, in the worshiping community. Disposable communion kits also challenge the mystery of the sacrament, transforming the Lord's Supper into the Lord's Snack, streamlined for the sake of sanitation and convenience.

Likewise, such contemporary practices raise questions regarding the Reformation descriptions of the church as that community where "the Word of God is preached and the Sacraments rightly observed." Are the "traditional" communities of faith that consider utilizing these "elements" reflecting on the implications for an understanding of the nature of the church itself? Might they create a kind of "virtual church" or generic Christianity, with limited sense of identity, tradition, and theology? Such questions also relate to baptism and its place in the Christian community. Martin Marty once cited a comment by Steve Andrews, pastor of Kensington Community Church, "an evangelical Presbyterian congregation near Detroit,"

---

[8] William L. Lumpkin, *Baptist Confessions of Faith* (Valley Forge: Judson Press, 1974) 292.

[9] Ibid., 293.

We immerse adults to baptize them, but we also sprinkle adults if that's what they want. We baptize infants, but we also dedicate infants if people want that instead. We'll back-flip someone into the pool if that's what they really want. . . . We don't want baptism to become a barrier that would keep anyone from Christianity.[10]

What should be the church's response to hologram preaching, disposable communion kits, and other technological "signs of the times" in the Christian church?

First, some may embrace the technology, utilizing it to gain the attention of a generation of seekers, long indifferent or antagonistic to traditional religion. Those who do should at least give passing attention to the impact of the medium upon the message. What, indeed, is the meaning of incarnation for congregations who gather around a preacher who is only virtually present and who only seems to be real? What is the necessity of the Eucharist prepared in pop-tab containers of temperance grape juice?

Second, those who anticipate these developments as possible ecclesiastical "trends" in the new millennium might well consider other communities that have dealt with these questions in other ways. Take, for example, the Society of Friends, the Quakers, who, three centuries ago, eschewed all outward sacraments and preaching for the inner light of God's Word hidden in the human heart. Quakers believed that Word and sacrament had been obscured by verbiage and ritual in the churches of seventeenth-century England. They resolved to "wait on the Lord" in silent worship, discovering an inner immersion into Christ, feeding on him, not in bread and cup, but in the sanctuary of their own hearts. Strangely, Quaker spirituality also produced some articulate preachers like George Fox, John Woolman, and Mary Dyer, the latter martyred by New England Puritans in 1660. Quakers precipitated a revival of mystical, transcendent faith. They were a real presence in their opposition to slavery, war, and poverty in England and America. Theirs was an important emphasis on incarnation, even as they spiritualized and internalized the outward sacraments.

Finally, proponents and critics of these new measures could recall another of the church's ancient tenets: The belief that Word and sacrament are *ex opere operato* ("from the work done"). Word and

---

[10] Martin E. Marty, "Memo," *Christian Century* (1–8 July 1998): 663.

sacrament exercise an intrinsic grace beyond the form or the administrator. In the mystery of faith, individuals will, no doubt, hear and believe through sermons delivered via hologram and through the Eucharistic moment shared with pull-top plastic. The possibility of such a miracle, however, should not obscure the church's calling to distinguish medium from message and its constant prayer for the wisdom to know the difference.[11]

---

[11] At the time this essay was written, "Remembrance" packets were under recall due to sanitary sealing problems. They continue to be used, particularly in large Protestant gatherings.

# To Do the Gift:
## Inaugural Lecture

*For Molly Marshall, President of Central Baptist Theological Seminary*

Johnny Cash and St. Paul set the stage for this auspicious moment. Not long before his death, Cash was interviewed on Terry Gross's program, *Fresh Air*, on National Public Radio. It was a wonderful, poignant event in which Johnny talked about his life and his long relationship with the late June Carter Cash, his beloved wife and musical collaborator. He also commented on his friendship with Elvis Presley and their early concerts together. He recalled his first hit, "I'll Walk the Line," and how it felt to be famous as a wide-eyed twenty-year-old. Gross asked if those first years of fame and "accolades" were hard to deal with. "Yes," Cash replied, "I was a country boy and there were times I wanted to go back to the farm." "But," he quickly added, "I had to do the gift." For many people who hear Johnny Cash's rough and raspy, slightly off-key voice, "the gift" may not seem all that important. But it stood the test of time. Whatever others might think of him and his music, Johnny Cash had to do the gift—to the end.[1]

Today, at the installation of a new president, we wonder again what it means to "do the gift" in Christian ministry. St. Paul said it could happen in his letter to the Corinthians: "There are varieties of gifts, but the same spirit. There are varieties of service, but the same Lord. There are varieties of activity, but in all of them and in everyone the same God is active. In each of us the Spirit is seen to be at work for some useful purpose." Whatever else a seminary might be, it is surely a place where gifts are explored, discerned and lived out.

It is a calling "to do the gift" that brings President Marshall to this moment in this place, on this evening. I have known Dr. Molly Marshall for almost thirty years as student, minister, colleague, scholar, friend, and teacher. Tonight, I am honored to celebrate her installation as

---

[1] "Johnny Cash: In His Own Words" *Fresh Air* from WHYY, November 24, 2005 (originally aired November 4, 1997).

president of this historic Baptist institution. But, like thousands of individuals across the American South and increasingly across the Midwest, I know President Marshall as Molly, a woman who, like Cher, has only a first name. I kid you not. Go into any group of former students who attended the Southern Baptist Theological Seminary in the decades of the '80s and '90s and simply say "Molly" and no one—I mean no one—will ask "Molly who?". We all know who Molly is. Why? Because she is infamous and famous all at once, celebrated and damned by Baptists here and there, then and now. But that is not the only reason. We know Molly because she has claimed so much of our history in struggling with Baptist life, identity, dissent, and discovery. We know Molly because, as our old friend, the late Dr. Kenneth Chafin used to say: "The people you run the rapids with, especially through the white water rapids, are your friends for life." A mutual friend of ours said to me recently: "So, is it true you've been asked to give the eulogy at Molly's installation as president of Central Seminary?" "No," I replied, lots of people thought they were giving the eulogy for a lot of things Molly has done among Baptists and not one of them has succeeded. That's what I'm going to celebrate!"

Likewise, at her request, this address is less President Marshall's pilgrimage, than about our common journey to "do the gift" with her, St. Paul, and Johnny Cash. But here at the start let me turn to my friend and simply offer my own profound congratulations and jubilation at this historic moment we observe here tonight. And let me turn to you and say without hesitancy: Molly is one of the most courageous human beings I have ever known in my life. I have seen that courage bubble up at moments when others hightailed it in the other direction. I have heard it in her sermons, seen it bear fruit in her students, and benefited from its powerful example of prophetic Christian witness in a sometimes-hostile world. Molly, I am grateful for your friendship, but I am changed, made stronger, by your courage, exemplified across the years and now carrying you to the future in this good place.

And what of the rest of us? What reflections on "doing the gift" might apply to each of us at a transitional moment such as this inauguration? Well, perhaps we consider the "art of ministry" that confronts us all, clergy and laity alike. A friend of mine who teaches at North Carolina School of the Arts once told me about a film editor's guide called *In the Blink of an Eye*, written by Walter Murch, a classic book that delineates the art of film editing.[2] The book suggests that film, indeed, many of the arts, includes three important components: Passion, Story, and Rhythm. Tonight, I would like to echo that assertion, with particular attention to the art of ministry and apply these three facets to our calling to do the gift of a new thing.

On the way to the future, we ask: What passions brought you to this place? Was it a passion for learning, mission, witness, conscience, social justice, racial reconciliation, feminist and gender voice, or care of souls? Passion has many meanings, from "any powerful emotion," to "ardent adoring love," to "boundless enthusiasm," to the threatening "martyrdom." Religion without passion isn't much religion; but religion with passionate excesses is downright dangerous. Sometime passion defines the non-negotiable elements of our lives—the ideas or commitments we cling to, come what may. Sometimes it marks the intensity of our learning. Sometime it simply wears us out. Passion for faith and learning should shape the days ahead at Central Seminary.

Passions for life and gospel shape us dramatically, don't they? They do in me. I am a Texan and a Baptist; I am required to be passionate about ideas, conscience, chips and salsa, and beef barbeque (not that rancid North Caroline pork substitute). We Texans demand passionate preaching to be sure. My Texas Baptist Grandmother taught me about passion in the pulpit with her two-sentence evaluation of the preacher: "He don't sweat; I don't listen."

Passionate Baptists were present from the beginnings of the movement. Written in 1648, Anglican Daniel Featley's critique of early British Baptists captures the passion of their dissenting ways:

> They preach, and print, and practice their heretical impieties openly; they hold their conventicles weekly in our chief cities, and suburbs thereof, and there prophesie by turnes; and...they build one another in the faith of their sect, to the ruin of their souls; they flock in great multitudes to their Jordans, and both sexes enter into the river, and are dipt after their manner with a kind of spell containing the heads of their erroneous tenets.... And as they defile our rivers with their impure washings, and our pulpits with their false prophecies and fanatical enthusiasms, so the presses sweat and groan under the load of their blasphemies.[3]

---

[2] Walter Murch, *In the Blink of an Eye: A Perspective on Film Editing* (New York: Silman-James Press, 2001).

[3] Bill J. Leonard, *Baptist Ways: A History* (Valley Forge: Judson Press, 2003) 51.

If we needed it, our forbearers gave us historical permission to live out our passions for the gospel. Passions bubble up readily in seminaries and divinity schools. Faculty and students bring their passions for scripture and theology, ministry and mission, into dialogue, struggling together for individual and collective voice. Some of our passions coincide, parallel, and unite us in common commitments. Others are diametrically opposed to each other, occupy either end of theological and cultural spectrums, a palpable dissent that challenges us to learn to talk to each other amid differences; critique ideas without attacking character; and listen TO each other rather than speak AT each other.

We academics often contend that learning at its best informs and even tempers passion. Reason and intellectual rigor, at their best, do not water down passion but keep it from becoming intolerant fanaticism. To be true to ourselves, we must ever hold our passions up to the light of intellectual discipline and the give and take of research and critical analysis. There is a thin line between passionate conviction and fanatical enthusiasm. Discerning the difference, especially these days in American society, is extremely difficult. I think it is worth the struggle, however, to claim our passions in the text, the church, and in the world.

Few of us, however, can be passionate about everything unless we live on double espressos hour by hour. We simply can't sustain unending passion about all things religious. Ministers who intend to be prophetically passionate about every issue had best work out a life-long relationship with U-Haul. For better or for worse, theological education helps us sort out our deepest passions and strongest concerns in the context of intellectual rigor and communal responsibility. To do the gift in ministry is to own and inform our passion for God, the world and other things.

Passion draws us to the story and the stories, doesn't it? To do the gift, to explore the art of ministry for the future, is to discover and rediscover, tell and retell the biblical stories. Indeed, the Bible is full of stories about people who get passionate, in every sense of the word, about life, religion, sin, and ideas, and act or act out accordingly.

Texts biblical and historical tell stories that invite us in and frighten us away. They conjure up images that haunt us in distinct and powerful ways. Just listen to a few and see what images they bring to mind ever so briefly:

- "And the man said, 'We heard the sound of you in the garden and we were afraid and we hid ourselves because we were naked.'"
- "And he called the woman Eve, because she was the mother of all who live."
- "And Moses tended the flock of Jethro in the back side of the desert."
- "And Sarah laughed when she heard this and said, 'How is it that I will have a child since I am out of my time and my husband is old?'"
- "The light that enlightens everyone has come into the world."
- "And the disciples returned and were surprised to find him talking to a woman."
- "Everyone usually serves the good wine first, and then the inferior wine after the guests have become drunk. But you have kept the best until last."
- "God from God, true God from true God, begotten not made, of one substance with the Father."—Nicene Creed
- "Thou hast made us for thyself and our hearts are restless till they rest in thee."—Augustine
- "The God who forgives us is father, mother and spouse."—Julian of Norwich
- "My conscience is captive to the Word of God and I Cannot and will not recant, for to go against conscience is neither safe nor right. God help me here I stand, Amen."—Martin Luther
- "I went to a congregation in Aldersgate street where one was reading from Luther's preface to the Romans, at a quarter before nine when he was reading of the change which God works in the heart by faith I felt my heart was strangely warmed, and I felt I did trust Christ for my salvation and an assurance was given me that he had taken away my sins and freed me from the law of sin and death."—John Wesley
- "Can you ever forgive me, my dear Nancy, when I tell you that I have become a Baptist."—Ann Hasseltine Judson
- "Some say that women cannot have as much rights as a man because Christ was not a woman; I ask you, where did Christ come from? From God and a woman, man had nothing to do with it. If the first woman God ever made was strong enough to turn the world upside down then all women together should be able to turn it right side up and now that they are asking to do it, the men better let them."—Sojourner Truth.

Stories haunt us, stalk us, draw us close and push us away. These days, I find myself haunted by the stories in the Bible. For a long time they did not haunt me because I was distracted by battles over theories regarding the text—so biblical inerrancy and the historical critical method both kept me from the text, fooled me into thinking that the text can, in David Tracy's words, be "domesticated," when it really cannot. Tracy insists that, "ancient texts resist domestication." They will not let us civilize them try as we might.

To do the gift in our time or any time is to be haunted by the stories and the texts. It is to retell and revisit the text, letting it go in ways wonderful and disturbing. As I said, these days I am haunted by certain texts moving beyond theories, beyond dogmas, to the messiness of the text.

Jesus' experience in the synagogue at Nazareth is a case in point, worthy of reflection by theological students and would-be ministers. In the passage provided in Luke 4, Jesus comes home and "as was his practice" shows up for Sabbath worship. They hand him the scroll and he reads out the word of God from the prophet Isaiah: "The Spirit of the Lord is upon me, because he has anointed me, he has sent me to announce good news to the poor, to proclaim release for prisoners and recovery of sight for the blind; to let the broken victims go free, to proclaim the year of the Lord's favour" (New English Bible). He returns the scroll to the attendant, sits down and says: "This day, this text has been fulfilled in your hearing." They are thrilled at his "gracious words," and ask, "Is this Joseph's son?" He then takes the text and turns it on them, challenging their theological correctness, and by the time he has finished, the people who have known him the longest but who understand him the least have turned against him and are prepared to throw him off a cliff. Let that story be a lesson to everyone of us inside or on the way to ministry in Christ's church. The same crowd that praises you will come for you shortly thereafter.

We tell stories and they find us and reshape us every day. Yet we dare not try to write ourselves into every story for some do not and will never belong to us. To claim every story is to have none, really. Sometime I think I have no right to retell some, maybe all, of the biblical stories because I have so little in common with the people of the text. I am so far from their world that it is silly at best and arrogant at worst to try to articulate them. So, perhaps one way to ease into that is to ask if they articulate me in any way. What are the common and uncommon hurts, sins, and vulnerabilities that bridge the centuries and link us in some strange even spiritual ways?

We must also bring our stories under the microscope of analysis and critique. The stories haunt us, but we cannot write ourselves into every story lest we really own none. My colleague and fellow Texan Mark Jensen, our professor of pastoral care at Wake Forest Divinity School, reminded me recently that part of our task is to struggle with students in developing, nurturing, and experiencing critical distance from the stories and ideas we study here. Critical distance means we do not write ourselves into every story but seek, at least at points, to step back, look over the fences that divide us, and work toward particular kinds of analysis and critique of stories ancient and modern, personal and communal. We look for tools to sort out and reflect on the meanings of the stories we tell and the glasses we use to read them.

And then there is rhythm. To do the gift is to seek what is, in the artist's words, "rhythmically satisfying." The idea of rhythm in art and ministry—art of ministry—is not to have everything in sync all the time, not to make everything fit, but to find ways of holding things in paradox, tension, struggle, frustration, and celebration and getting on with or at least coping with life. To do the gift is to move into and struggle against the rhythms of life. Midsummer last year I received an email from one of our graduates who commented that while she was glad not to be taking tests, glad to be graduated, she would miss the rhythms of life in the divinity school and the university. And I don't think she simply meant that she would miss the schedules. I think she meant the rhythms of the spirit that she had found in the blessing and benefits, stresses and strains of our ever vulnerable academic and spiritual community—ways of ordering existence, marking time, measuring our days, and collecting (literally) our thoughts. At best, (and we may not always hit the mark on this) we provide a safe, but challenging place to explore these ideas of faith, hope, gospel, reason, revelation, intellect, spirit, sin, life and death. Rhythm is the way we hold those deep personal and intellectual struggles together or at least in tension.

Academics do that too, I hope. To anticipate the rhythms of the text is to begin with hermeneutics—the glasses we wear when we read texts—rather than theories of inspiration or critical tools. We may get to those theories and tools, but we do not begin with them. We crawl down into the text as see where it might take us at that moment when the world seems most broken, most vulnerable, most in need of some word from God. Is it too much to say that it is less that we exegete the text than that we let the text exegete us—perhaps with multiple readings and possibilities. It is attempting to let the text examine us even as we attempt to examine the text. To seek the rhythms of the text is to acknowledge that it is multilayered with multiple possibilities, personal, historical, linguistic, and communal, and then lean toward one way of clinging to it for dear life.

This is of course dangerous because it can be too subjective, too individualistic, too pop, too hokey, too uninformed—so we have to know the dangers and do our homework. If necessary, we also might try to find some serious boundaries that help us navigate the hazards. One way is to make sure that the seminary and ultimately church, is a safe, but challenging place (is that asking the impossible?) to explore these ideas of faith, hope, gospel, reason, revelation, intellect, spirit, sin, life, and death. Rhythm is the way in which we hold those deep personal and intellectual struggles together, or at least in tension. At their best, early Baptist congregations mirrored that appreciation for conscience and voice, with a Biblicism and theological diversity that took them in a variety of directions, Arminian and Calvinist, later conservative and liberal, missionary and non-missionary—contradictory hermeneutics inside historic Baptist identity. At their worst they succumbed all too easily to theological warfare, character assassination, and ecclesiastical schism.

Another such safe place could be the liturgical rhythms of the Christian year. In a sense the Christian year marks the rhythms of the church, an annual cycle of events that retells the story of Jesus and reclaims our own stories. Advent's expectations move to Christmas fulfillment. Lent marks the journey of reflection on a story that becomes increasingly dissonant. The rhythm of Holy Week is the Way of the Cross punctuated by chaos, betrayal, and encounter with the Crucified God. The rhythm of Easter is the sound and fury of resurrection and unanticipated joy, tempered quickly by the realities of a reactionary world, until Pentecost claims a new community where old ones see visions and young ones dream dreams, AND WOMEN SPEAK, PREACH AND PROPHESY with the same courage and inspiration that kept them at the cross and made them the first bearers of the news of resurrection.

In the book, *Jayber Crow*, Wendell Berry writes about a small Kentucky town called Port William where the preachers in the local Baptist church come from the theological seminary in the nearby city. There are only semi-permanent, part-time ministers. Jayber says of them: "The preachers were always young students from the seminary who wore, you might say, the mantle of power but not the mantle of knowledge. They wouldn't stay long enough to know where they were."[4] Whatever is it, the "mantle of knowledge"? Reading Wendell Berry, I don't think it means simply "head knowledge" although it surely means a quest for learning at its best. But it also means "knowing" something of life, something of people, and something of ourselves.

But Jayber gives us some hope, has the last word, I suppose, when he acknowledges that "a few of those young preachers were bright and could speak—I mean they were troubled enough in their own hearts to have something to say. A few had wakefully read some books." Great words. So through the passions, the stories and the rhythms of life, are you troubled enough in your own hearts TO HAVE SOMETHING TO SAY? If so, have some passion about it, for God's sake, for GOD'S sake. Amen.

---

[4] Wendell Berry, *Jayber Crow* (New York: Counterpoint, 2001) 160.

# Losing Privilege, Regaining Voice:
## Southern Religion in a New Community[1]

## Beloved Community Lectures

On 17 January 2012, the Supreme Court of the United States refused to hear an appeal from the Forsyth County, North Carolina, Board of Commissioners regarding a lower court's ruling that supported an end to deity-specific, sectarian-oriented prayers at Commissioners' meetings. The case originated when the American Civil Liberties Union sued the Commissioners for permitting such prayers at the opening of their meetings. Although the prayers are voluntary—ministers choose to sign up for the occasion—the majority of prayers end in "Jesus' name," a fact that ACLU lawyers said showed government favoritism to one religion over another. Opponents, represented by the Alliance Defense Fund, insisted that these efforts constituted a denial of religious liberty to those who chose to pray out of their specific traditions. Two regional courts ruled against the county, decisions settled by the Supreme Court's refusal to continue hearing the case. At a news conference, a Forsyth County minister noted that the decision "creates a chilling effect on religious speech in America," and the local newspaper reported his concern that the courts' ruling "penalizes the county for being largely Christian. Pluralism found its way into Forsyth County, North Carolina.

In 2011, while giving lectures at a local North Carolina ministers' group I was approached by a mid-career minister from a very traditional Southern Baptist Church who asked: "Do you think people will ever come back to Sunday School the way they once did?" The sociology of Sunday has found its way into churches that thought things would never change.

At a recent alumni lunch, a thirty-something seminary graduate expresses the fear that his entire left-leaning denomination will not endure until he can get to retirement. A local pastor calls to say that the

[1] This address was presented as part of the Beloved Community Lectures at Mercer University, Macon GA, 9 February 2012.

sentiment at his evangelical denomination's annual meeting is the hope that it can last one more year.

Religion in the American South is changing, and even the preachers know it. While traditional elements appear outwardly unscathed, major transitions lie just beneath the cultural surface. The second decade of the twenty-first century reflects the rapid decline of Protestant privilege in America at large, and the South in particular. While Christians remain the distinct majority, secularism, pluralism, and religious diversity (even in the hinterlands) is changing the religious and political landscape of the region. Today there are many Southern religions—regional, theological, liturgical, economic, and political. Southern religion includes black Roman Catholics, Jesus-only Pentecostals, and biblical inerrantists as diverse asm Southern Baptists and Appalachian serpent-handlers. There are Strict Calvinist Two-Seed-in-the-Spirit Predestinarian Baptists, as well as the more Arminian-oriented Church of the Nazarene. Today's South is comprised of big steeple and storefront churches, emerging and mega-churches, Buddhist meditation groups, Namaste Yoga classes, neighborhood mosques, home Bible studies, Twelve-Step groups, and NASCAR rallies, all with varying expressions of religious intensity.

While references to America as a "Christian Commonwealth" abound throughout the nation's history, the phrase "Judeo-Christian nation" is relatively new. Martin Marty dates the earliest use of the term to 1899, concluding that, "it certainly did not enter the argot of America until World War II."[2] Even with increased immigration, Jews and Judaism were not easily admitted into the pantheon of American religion and culture, as evidenced in formal and informal restrictions required of Jews in schools, private clubs, and the workplace. [3]

Acceptance of Roman Catholics into American religious life was a long time coming, symbolized perhaps in 1960 with the election of John F. Kennedy, and further reflected today in a majority of Supreme Court justices. Although Catholics are the largest religious tradition in the US, anti-Catholic sentiments endure even as Evangelicals and Catholics join forces in defending certain shared values and supporting conservative

---

[2] Martin E. Marty, *Modern American Religion: Under God Indivisible, 1941–1960* (Chicago: University of Chicago Press, 1996) 332.

[3] The 1947 film, *A Gentleman's Agreement*, documents the public and private responses to Jews in World War II America.

presidential candidates.[4] Early America is best understood as a "Protestant nation" rather than a Judeo-Christian one. Protestant hegemony generally endured well into the twentieth century.

Will Herberg's classic study, *Protestant, Catholic, Jew,* published in 1955, was one of the earliest scholarly claims that America had become a "melting pot" of religious pluralism as evidenced in the confluence of three great faiths. Nonetheless, the sociologist fretted over the rising secularism he observed in mid-twentieth-century American life. He urged the three great traditions to reassert their own distinct identities even as they learned to work together in a new cooperative pluralism. Herberg concluded:

> America was once almost entirely Protestant; the transformation of Protestant America into the tripartite America of the "triple melting pot" has taken place, in a measure, through its union with two minority communities very different in ethnic and social composition. Present-day America reflects, at almost every point, the basic fact of its history.[5]

If Herberg pressed the "melting pot" idea too far, he anticipated a new pluralism that was extended to non-Protestant groups who shared Judeo-Christian roots. It involved the recognition that Jews and Catholics had come of age in American life, evident in growing numbers and greater public acceptance. Marty cites Jewish professor Seymour Martin Lipset's observation that "mainstream Protestants, who were yielding their old claims to monopoly or hegemony and learning to share space and power with others, evidently began to use Judeo-Christian language in order to sound American and to abandon claims for superiority."[6] New immigrant communities including Muslims, Hindus, Buddhists, and lesser known "spiritualties," create new challenges for certain Protestant traditionalists who sense their influence waning, wrenched away from them by an increasingly pluralistic, secular society where religious liberty tends to make the religious ground more level than it has ever been before.

These realities did not appear overnight. Students of American religion have documented their progression for decades. Historian

---

[4] Bob Allen, "Pressler denies Santorum endorsement was rigged," *The Christian Century* (18 January 2012).
[5] Will Herberg, *Protestant, Catholic, Jew* (Garden City: Anchor Books, 1955) 211.
[6] Marty, *Modern American Religion*, 333.

Samuel Hill, Jr., friend and teacher to many of us, describes certain "common assumptions" or "conventional wisdom" regarding the nature of Southern religion. His list is instructive in light of present transitions. First, he notes that popular religion in the South generally revealed various styles of "conservative Protestantism." This included sectarian Pentecostal communions, as well as denominationally oriented Methodists and Baptists. Second, Hill writes that, "the biracial nature of historic southern society is universally acknowledged as a crucial factor in the society's religious life, as much so as in any other aspect."[7] Hill and other scholars detailed the relationship between the South's "two cultures," black and white, from slavery through segregation to the civil rights era.[8] Third, certain religious practices—revivalistic, evangelical, pietistic, and experiential—that persisted in Southern churches are now declining or experiencing major alterations. While these religious qualities were evident in other regions, they take on a special character in the South. Fourth, cultural and regional insulation helped to shape the nature of religion in the region. Throughout much of the twentieth century, Southern culture provided something of a cocoon that insulated religion in the region. Fifth, Hill suggests that the region has been characterized by what might be called a "pervasive evangelicalism," incorporating personal religious experience, biblical authority, and proselytizing missionary zeal.[9]

This style of Christianity creates an environment in which sects (sex too for that matter) flourish and where religious dissent and establishmentarian status quo exist side by side. Indeed, in the South there is a tendency toward both sectarian rhetoric and establishment institutionalism, religious people who talk like Democrats and act like Republicans or vice versa. That is, many churches in the South talk the language of sectarianism—dissent, conscience, radical conversion, rigorous ethical code, millennial expectation, while at the same time identifying with establishmentarian, privileged policies in relation to government, politics, education and public morality. Beneath the rhetoric of dissent is a strong commitment toward preserving the cultural status quo.

---

[7] Samuel S. Hill, Jr., ed., *Varieties of Southern Religious Experience* (Baton Rouge: Louisiana State University Press, 1980) 211.

[8] Samuel S. Hill, Jr., *Religion and the Solid South* (Nashville: Abingdon Press, 1972) 24–56.

[9] Hill, Jr., *Varieties of Southern Religious Experience*, 213.

Slavery and segregation clearly illustrate this dichotomy. Generations of pious slaveholders and segregationists used the language of liberation to call people to salvation, but refused to apply spiritual liberation to cultural practice. Likewise, many white Christians linked biblical authority with racial subjugation, suggesting that if the Bible was wrong in its sanction of slavery and segregation, it also might be wrong on the resurrection of Jesus Christ and life in the world to come.

Writing in the 1970s, that profile of Southern religion led Martin Marty to describe Southern Protestantism—especially the Southern Baptist Convention—as one of the most "intact" religious subcultures in modern America. Such intactness meant that a religious group exercised continuity with its past, and provided a unifying sense of identity for its constituents in the present. In Marty's words, it revealed "regularities of behavior and consistent norms for evaluation."[10] Intactness meant that religious groups, Protestant and Southern, black and white, were held together by common cultural, organizational, and religious experiences.

Decades later, however, scholars trace the loss of regional intactness and the impact on broad national trends on Southern religious life and institutions. Sociologist Wade Clark Roof cites John Shelton Reed's comment that there may be an "enduring South," but it is neither static nor unchanging.[11] Indeed, Roof concludes that, "no longer can an intact southern religious culture be simply assumed."[12]

Clearly religion in the South, like other aspects of Southern regionalism, has become more generically American year after year. The South, like other regions, is impacted by what might be called the Wal-Martization of the American nation in which everything from shopping centers to social media contribute to a generic mass culture, evident from coast to coast. (Tractor pulls remain a small exception, however.)

In spite of this, Roof insists that, "religion in Dixie is still characterized by high visibility, strong conservatism, and moral traditionalism."[13] He suggests that despite mass trends "there is still a

---

[10] Martin E. Marty, "The Protestant Experience and Perspectives," in *American Religious Values and the Future of America* (Philadelphia: Fortress Press, 1978) 40.

[11] Hill, Jr., *Varieties of Southern Religious Experience*, 208.

[12] Ibid.

[13] Wade Clark Roof, "Religious Change in the American South: The Case of the Unchurched," in *Varieties of Southern Religious Experience* (Baton Rouge: Louisiana State University Press, 1980) 197.

definite regional religious ethos and style" in the South.[14] He adds that, "what is truly remarkable about the South, and the Sun Belt generally, is that, though it welcomes new technologies and new migrants, regional ideologies and loyalties are not seriously undermined."[15]

Religion in the contemporary South is at once similar and distinct when compared to the broader cultural context. The old traditions still frame religious identity, but they are fast being overtaken by powerful forces of regional, cultural, and theological pluralism, all with significant impact on traditional Southern Protestantism.

Such cultural transitions parallel those of our frontier forebears at the beginning of the nineteenth century. In that day, the forces of democracy and freedom reshaped irrevocably the religious and political life in the new nation. Religious liberty meant the death of old European-born ecclesiastical establishments, and churches, particularly on the frontier, searched for new ways to organize themselves and fulfill their mission amid newfound religious freedom and democratic idealism. In response they created organizational and theological mechanisms evident in denominational systems and revivalistic conversionism. Thus the denomination became the chief method for organizing American churches. Cultural transition influenced theological revisionism as religious communities turned away from older emphases on divine sovereignty, predestination, and election to greater concern for free will, individualism, and democratic participation in everything from church government to personal salvation. Revivals called people to be saved and told them how to do so. Protestants won the battle for the frontier, securing religious privilege that shaped public religion for generations, a legacy now less viable in the face of secularism, pluralism, scholasticism, propositionalism, modernity, and postmodernity. Can religious Americans reshape religious life as creatively as did their nineteenth-century forebears? Current studies chart the loss of old hegemonies here and now.

In the book *American Grace: How Religion Divides and Unites Us*, published in 2010, Donald Campbell and Robert Putnam collected data from religious surveys and polling profiles taken from the 1960s to around 2008. The profile includes:

---

[14] Ibid.
[15] Ibid., 192.

- Mainline Protestants now stand at no more than thirteen percent of the American population and continue to decline.
- Roman Catholics, the country's largest religious group, maintain their status largely through immigration given the rapid departure of large numbers of "Anglo-Catholics" from the church.
- Evangelicals peaked in the 1990s and currently seem plateaued at some twenty-five percent of the population.
- The so-called "nones," those who repudiate any religious commitment or membership—though long present in American life—now seem ready to own that designation in national polls, jumping from around 7 to 15 percent in the past three to five years.[16]

Given these sociological realities, what profiles of Southern religion lie ahead? First, in terms of constituency, Southern churches confront an expanding number of "nones" who are outside or who have dropped out of religious institutions. Churches, thus, must take seriously a growing and much-overlooked subgroup in the South: The unchurched.

In an earlier study, Wade Clark Roof compared churched and unchurched individuals in the region. Unchurched involved those who do not belong to a church or synagogue, or who had not attended such institutions within the previous six months apart from major religious holidays. His investigation suggests that while the South had the smallest number of unchurched persons when compared to other regions, the East, Midwest, and West, the difference is not substantial.

Unchurched persons represented 41 percent in the South, 45 percent in the East, 43 percent in the Midwest, and 53 percent in the West. Roof concluded that "the degree of similarity of southern and nonsouthern patterns is striking; there appears to be little demographic basis for believing that there are widespread differences between the southern and non-southern unchurched."[17] Thus, in spite of its religious infrastructure, the Southern profile of non-affiliation looks surprisingly similar to that of the rest of the nation.

In the South, as elsewhere, many unchurched persons continue to maintain personal religious beliefs while abandoning relationships with the institutional church. Roof observes that a growing number of Americans seem to be "believers but not belongers" when it comes to

---

[16] Robert D. Putnam and David E. Campbell, *American Grace: How Religion Divides and Unites Us* (New York: Simon & Schuster, 2010) 103–13.

[17] Roof, "Religious Change in the American South," 196.

institutional religion.[18] Roof's research, like that of Princeton sociologist Robert Wuthnow, gives preliminary credence to another facet of the "two-culture" theory of Southern society. Whereas earlier analysts applied the two-culture idea to black and white subgroups in the South, newer studies reflect the growth of two broader cultures, one secular, the other traditionally religious. These early investigations show that even in the South the gap between "churched and unchurched is substantial."[19] Roof writes that the South may soon become the region most ideally situated for studying cultural and religious polarization in America, in which case there will be little doubt that the cultural bonds linking Southerners and religion will have broken."[20]

Second, it is clear that a significant transition is underway among the so-called churched constituency in the South, particularly where denominational affiliation is concerned. Sociologists and historians generally agree that fewer religious folk in America in general, and the South in particular, perceive their primary religious identity in terms of a specific denomination.[21] Indeed, growing numbers of religious persons are apt to affiliate with churches based on peculiar programs and services rendered than out of loyalty to a specific denominational tradition. Younger people seem particularly more willing to "switch" from one religious group to another in order to meet specified needs at a given time in their lives. Many seem more willing to move on to another faith communion if they feel it provides better response to their ever-changing life situations. Likewise, racial, ecumenical, and interfaith marriage may represent the stealth bomber of American pluralism, creating a familial diversity that makes sectarian privilege difficult to support and sustain.

When it comes to a changing constituency, therefore, Southern churches face a society in which the number of nonaffiliated is increasing, where members have a more "fluid" sense of denominational and interfaith identity, and where religious consumerism sets a powerful agenda with far-reaching institutional and theological implications.

---

[18] Ibid., 199.
[19] Ibid., 205.
[20] Ibid., 209.
[21] Wade Clark Roof and William McKinney, *American Mainline Religion* (New Brunswick NJ: Rutgers University Press, 1987) 244–49.

The tendency toward individualism and privatization in all areas of life, including religion, is a major challenge for religious communions. As denominational loyalties decline, and persons move in and out of specific denominational and religious subgroups, churches must find new ways to establish, develop, and nurture Christian community. While the Christian gospel clearly has individual implications, Christian faith is difficult to sustain outside such signs of Christian community as *ecclesia*, Body of Christ, people of God, family of faith. At the same time, changing realities in contemporary culture mean that churches must reevaluate the way in which community gathers for worship, prayer, study, and mission.

Any discussion of the future of Christian community and institutions in the South cannot overlook the role of the so-called mega-churches now exercising a powerful ecclesiastical presence in the region. Mega-churches are those congregations that not only manifest a membership of several thousand persons, but also seek to provide a wide variety of ministries and specialized services for a diverse constituency. In a sense, mega-churches are mini-denominations offering through one congregation services—education, mission, publishing, small groups—that previously came through denominational networks.

This supply-side approach to the mission and ministry of the church portends the development of shopping center pragmatism in ecclesiastical life. It offers persons an opportunity to choose a church based certain services rendered and develops ministries through effective marketing techniques. Southern churches of all sizes now feel increasing pressure to accept or respond to the mega-church agenda, adapting ministries and services to specific constituencies, creating a variety of *ecclesiolae in ecclesia*, little churches within the church, to respond to the needs and preferences of specific subgroups.

Southern churches now give less attention to denominational structure than to regional and local configurations in which churches pick and choose what special missions, ministries and activities in which they participate or support financially. This loss of denominational loyalty creates a significant loss of denominational hegemony in the South. Denominations find it difficult to fund traditional programs, draw constituents to annual conferences, and address cultural issues with the same influence they once manifested. Instead, congregational localism has become the chief source of ecclesial identity for a growing number of Christians across the theological and denominational spectrum.

Mega-churches, the decline of denominational identity, the expansion of regionalism, and localism in missionary endeavor means that Southern churches also confront major theological challenges in the next century. In light of changing organizational structures, perhaps one essential question is how will the churches pass on a tradition? Is there such a thing as generic Christianity cut off from the tradition of the church as well as from historical specificity? Are non-denominational, mega-churches able to pass on a tradition to succeeding generations, or are they simply this year's new religious shopping mall, organized around a programmed obsolescence, bypassed by the next new mega-church offering newer and better shops and services to the next generation of convert/consumers?

In responding to such questions we might turn to issues of theology and spirituality in the future of Southern religion. By the early decades of the twenty-first-century theological liberals and conservatives alike seem unable to provide meaningful response to the spiritual concerns of our time. For roughly the last hundred years, modernism/liberalism and fundamentalism/evangelicalism developed as two sides of the same enlightenment coin. Both utilized enlightenment rationalism to interpret and respond to the onslaught of modernity. Their intellectual motifs belie the rationalism inherent in both their systems of thought. Liberals promoted the historical critical method and the effort to demythologize traditional religious ideas. Conservative evangelicals promoted Scottish Common Sense Realism and such recent ideas as creation science. Liberalism's attempts to demythologize scripture, theology, and doctrine have left many wondering what was really Christian in the end. Conservatives' concerns for the protection of old myths at all cost have led them dangerously close to a spiritless propositionalism that has maximized orthodoxy and minimized faith. Both have stressed the cognitive at the expense of the experiential, the rational at the expense of the spiritual.

Robert Ferm, professor of religion at Middlebury College, observes: "The Christian faith and Christian identity are not as simple as many would have us believe. Issues posed in debates between 'liberals' and 'fundamentalists' are no longer significant ones."[22] He believes that much American Protestantism has distorted "the assumption that fundamentally the Christian faith is a distinctive understanding of human nature and human redemption."[23] Ferm calls on the contemporary church to consider the gospel as "testimony to weakness and power, to deprivation and strength, to a costly global view of our common salvation without platitudes or painless pap."[24]

Theological debates carried into the public square call churches to consider their public "testimony." In a pluralistic society, conviction and conscience in a particular religious community may appear as bigotry in the larger society. Churches that declare their deepest convictions as a public witness may not be able to sustain culture dominance and should be willing to accept that reality.

At the same time, twenty-first-century Southern churches may be forced to choose between scholasticism and spirituality. In that process, Southern sinners, like other regional sinners, may turn from the cognitive to the experiential, seeking those religious movements that nurture transcendence and mystery, whether in the charismatic or the liturgical setting—perhaps both. In a sense, Southern religionists may be best suited for this quest since theirs is a legacy of personal religious experience. Sam Hill recognized that legacy when he wrote that: "The southern religious tradition has fruitful resources to tap, which it has failed to cultivate to its own benefit.... That is to say, southern people possess the personal history to enable them to encounter transcendence within ordinary experience, as the persons they are."[25] He concluded that "on both personal and societal fronts,...southerners are prototypical existentialists." For southerners "neither concepts nor traditions nor abstractions have governed the southern imagination, but events, transactions, relationships, feelings, and gratifications."[26] Until theological debates are tempered by a renewed spirituality, denominational and congregational unrest will no doubt continue.

---

[22] Robert L. Ferm, *Piety, Purity, Plenty: Images of Protestantism in America* (Minneapolis: Fortress Press, 1991) 117.
[23] Ibid, 8.
[24] Ibid, 116.
[25] Hill, Jr., *Religion and the Solid South*, 184.
[26] Ibid., 183.

This atmosphere of ecclesiastical uncertainty and theological scholasticism seems to have provoked a renewed concern for spirituality, what Quaker mystic Rufus Jones called "immediate awareness of relation to God, on direct and intimate consciousness of the Divine Presence."[27] While privatized religious experience has long characterized Southern religion, there is yet to be a significant movement of practical spirituality that incorporates personal religion with a clear-cut social imperative. Such spirituality might move churches beyond theological speculation and corpse-cold propositionalism, opening the door to issues of race, gender, the laity, and social action in Southern churches. Such spirituality will surely produce its own controversy, no doubt.

James Cone and other writers have long insisted that the movement for civil rights was nurtured in the spirituality of black churches across the South. Through a powerful religious experience, personal and communal, a people rose up to confront social inequities.[28] Is it too much to hope that a renewed spirituality of this sort will overtake Christian communities black and white, rich and poor, male and female, motivating and empowering them to work together in response to a new challenges of homelessness, poverty, family life, HIV/AIDS, drug abuse—an endless litany of complex and oppressive social ills which can only become more severe in the new century.

Given these historical and contemporary realities, how might Baptist progressivism on matters of conscience and dissent inform the future of an increasingly diverse, pluralistic, secular, global culture?

First, how might congregations become, in the words of Roger Williams and John Clarke, "a shelter for persons distressed of conscience" and a prophetic community that distresses the consciences of members and non-members alike in response to the great issues, ideas and injustices of our times? Might we determine to nurture a safe environment in the church and in the society where consciences are enlivened even as they collide?

Second, in an environment where pluralism and uncoerced faith are often taken for granted, how do we speak about faith and conscience, even dissent as a response to extreme sectarianism and tribalism, or

---

[27] Rufus Jones, *Studies in Mystical Religion* (London: McMillan, 1909) xv.
[28] James H. Cone: *Martin & Malcolm & America: A Dream or a Nightmare?* (Maryknoll NY: Orbis Books, 1991) 19–37, 120–50; and James Melvin Washington, *Frustrated Fellowship: The Black Baptist Quest for Social Power* (Macon GA: Mercer University Press, 1987).

secular and religious indifference? In a religiously volatile world, is it still important to discern, if not challenge, those implicit or explicit religio-political establishments that seek privilege and entitlement through sectarian or secular hegemony over politics, religion, educational institutions, and economics, economics, economics? Third, might a radical understanding of conscience encourage us to an equally radical concern for VOICE—an environment in which everyone can speak even when the differences are vast and irreconcilable? Fourth, in our quest for pluralism of voice, however, we must resist the temptation to syncretistic "politeness" that trivializes serious theological differences inside and outside the Christian fold. Some divisions over ideas and history cannot be fixed by easy dialogue and dismissive or paternalistic attitudes toward serious differences. But, if there is any Gospel hope at all, we can find ways to attack ideas without attacking character.

Finally, with the earlier generations of Christians, might we explore more explicitly the nature and boundaries of dissent in the face of such issues as mass culture, media religion, and the struggle for global resources? Such dissent might compel us to take a chance—stake our lives—on ideas that inform and overpower, even when we know they will never secure majoritarian approval. An example of that dissent in response to national and global issues was illustrated recently in a prophetic document written by the Rev. Maria Bonafede, moderator of the Tavola Valdense, a community of Waldensian Churches in Italy. Entitled "The Responsibility of a Minority," it expresses vigorous opposition to the efforts of the Italian government to fingerprint 80,000 Roma-Gypsy children in Italy, a mistaken attempt to respond to crime, anti-immigrant, and anti-gypsy sentiments in contemporary Italian society. Bonafede offers this powerful explanation for her opposition to this practice, words that capture brilliantly the reason why American Christians need to recover faith and conscience in an ever-expanding globalism. She writes:

> There are moments during which responsibility for vigorously affirming fundamental principles of civil society falls on the shoulders of small minorities. It is the duty of these minorities to intervene because they know firsthand the pain of prejudice and persecution inflicted by the majority, a majority all too often ill-informed, distracted, confused or manipulated and therefore unable to stop episodes of hatred, discrimination and violence against whomever's turn it is to be different.

Today it is the turn of the Gypsy children.... As Waldensians and Methodists, we acknowledge ourselves a minority that on the topic of civil rights has an important word to say. We speak, therefore, with all the strength and conviction at our disposal. We cannot keep silent during this moment when our spiritual, ethical and civil responsibility demand we speak out.[29]

Like our Waldensian and Methodist brothers and sisters in Italy and elsewhere, we have a historic opportunity, indeed, obligation to exercise "the responsibility of a minority," in our own culture, and for many of us, perhaps, in our own churches and sub-denominations, speaking out from the depth of Christ-arrested consciences against the "hatred, discrimination and violence" of our global communities. Wouldn't it be wonderful if in losing our cultural hegemony and privilege we recovered our voice, not as entitlement but as Gospel? World without end. Amen.

---

[29] Maria Bonafede, "The Responsibilities of a Minority," typescript, email to Bill J. Leonard, 30 June 2008.

# Vocation: Claiming and Being Claimed[1]

In 1836 a free black woman named Jarena Lee paid thirty-eight dollars to print a thousand copies of her autobiography entitled *The Life and Religious Experience of Jarena Lee, A Coloured Lady*, the first autobiography of a black woman to be published in America. In it she tells of her spiritual pilgrimage, beginning with her conversion in 1804 and her sanctification four years later through the influence of the fledgling African Methodist Episcopal Church, founded in 1787. She wrote:

> Between four and five years after my sanctification, on a certain time, an impressive silence fell upon me, and I stood as if someone was about to speak to me, yet I had no such thought in my heart. But to my utter surprise there seemed to sound a voice which I thought I distinctly heard, and most certainly understood, which said to me, "Go and preach the Gospel!" I immediately replied aloud, "No one will believe me." Again I listened, and again the same voice seemed to say, "Preach the Gospel; I will put words in your mouth, and will turn your enemies to become your friends."[2]

Many people, including Bishop Richard Lee, founder of the AME church, warned her against it, but she would not be deterred. In the end she concluded:

> In my wanderings up and down among men, preaching according to my ability, I have frequently found families who told me that they had not for several years been to a meeting, and yet, while listening to hear what God would say by this poor coloured female instrument have believed with trembling.[3]

In her nineteenth-century language and context "that poor coloured female instrument reflects something of the power of vocation in a

---

[1] This address was given at the annual meeting of the National Association of Baptist Professors of Religion, Gardner Webb University, 23 May 2011.
[2] William L. Andrews, *Sisters of the Spirit* (Bloomington: Indiana University Press, 1986) 35.
[3] Ibid., 37.

human life, a journey that knowingly or unknowingly, recognized or unrecognized, shapes us to this day.

Jarena Lee "got the call," discovering a sense of religious vocation, her identity as a Christian, a preacher, and a human being. By vocation I mean a sense of one's own identity in the world; a sense of self that informs who we are and shapes what we choose to do in life. A sense of vocation need not be faith-based, but for those who do claim faith, it is an opportunity to explore what Fredrick Buechner calls *Sacred Journey*. He writes: "Deep within history, as it gets itself written down in history books and newspapers, in the letters we write and the diaries we keep, is sacred history, is God's purpose working itself out in the apparent purposelessness of human history and our separate histories, is the history, in short of the saving and losing of souls, including our own."[4]

Vocation incorporates, informs, and moves beyond choosing a "profession," or finding a job. Indeed, in the course of our lives we may have multiple jobs and numerous professions, each of which may be informed by a sense of vocation. Thus, vocation is, as the Quakers suggest, that which "centers" you no matter what your role in the world or the church may be. Buechner gets at this brilliantly, I think, when he writes that we all come of age, understand ourselves, through "a dramatic moment" or more likely "moments so subtle and undramatic that we scarcely recognize them." This sacred journey, he insists, is "a journey *in search*...in which there will be as many answers as there are searchers, but perhaps there are certain general answers that will do for us all."[5]

Of this sense of identity Buechner concludes: "We search for a self to be. We search for other selves to love. We search for work to do." Those three pursuits shape our vocational quest. Then Buechner adds a touch of mystery to it all, writing: "And since even when to one degree or another we find these things, we find also that there is still something crucial missing which we have not found, we search for that unfound thing too, even though we do not know its name or where it is to be found or even if it is to be found at all."[6] If Buechner is correct, then the mystery of the search means that our vocation is always forming and

---

[4] Frederick Buechner, *The Sacred Journey* (San Francisco: Harper & Row, 1982) 4–5.
[5] Ibid., 58.
[6] Ibid.

never fully formed. We are both seekers and learners every day of our lives.

At its best, an "academic vocation" in a setting of higher education fosters learning and demands exploration of ideas, issues and actions that enlighten our sense of vocation, dare we say "calling."

Defining vocation is as diverse and as divided as the church itself. For Catholics, vocation is inseparable from the church's sacramental calling found in marriage and holy orders, both outward and visible signs of inward and spiritual grace. Marriage is the vocation of family, a calling to nurture a new generation of human beings in life and faith. Holy Orders are the vocation of service to God and church offered to and through male priests and other male and female "religious." Indeed, for Catholics past and present, the word vocation refers primarily to the practice of priestly calling and sacramental practice.

Yet even at his most "Catholic" point in life, Thomas Merton expands the sense of vocation, specifically to the role of the artist in the world. The *Seven Storey Mountain* draws the reader in from the opening paragraphs.

> On the last day of January 1915, under the sign of the Water Bearer, in a year of a great war, and down in the shadow of some French mountains on the borders of Spain, I came into the world. Free by nature, in the image of God, I was nevertheless the prisoner of my own violence and my own selfishness, in the image of the world into which I was born. That world was the picture of hell, full of men like myself, loving God and yet hating Him; born to love Him; living instead in fear and hopeless self-contradictory hungers.... My father and mother were captives in that world, knowing they did not belong with it or in it, and yet unable to get away from it. They were in the world and not of it—not because they were saints, but in a different way: because they were artists. The integrity of an artist lifts a man above the level of the world without delivering him from it.[7]

In a few short lines, Merton links his own birth with astrology, a World War, European geography, Augustinianism, and the aesthetic. He introduces his life even as he defines the nature of the artist—perhaps even the nature of vocation—in the world.

Merton wrote that true artists did not need "an ideal of freedom," but "freedom from the internalized emotional pressures by which

---

[7] Thomas Merton, *The Seven Storey Mountain* (New York: Signet Books, 1948) 9.

society holds" the artist down. This, he said, was the "freedom of conscience."[8] He concluded: "In the last analysis, the only valid witness to the artist's creative freedom is his [her] work itself. The artist builds his [her] own freedom and forms his [her] own artistic conscience, by the work of his [her] hands. Only when the work is finished can he [she] tell whether or not it was done 'freely.'"[9] Mystically, perhaps simply mythically, Merton's description of the artist's vocation/identity might also be applied to that of the academic—work that is both objective and subjective, born of issues related to freedom, conscience and the "witness" of the "work itself." I'm not sure about that; it may be far too sentimental, but I like the way it feels for Baptist reasons that I will discuss momentarily.

Five hundred years ago priest and professor Martin Luther redefined the nature of vocation, forging the Protestant Reformation, and splitting the church. Luther said we all have a vocation, as sure and certain as that of any priest. Vocation is the calling of every Christian to be the servant of Christ whatever our specific "work" in society. The mother washing dirty diapers at the sink had as important a calling, Luther said, as the priest consecrating the Eucharist at the altar. So Luther separated vocation—what every Christian is to cultivate in the world—from calling, the specific function of individuals in society.

John Calvin distinguishes between two "vocations" or callings, each with a salvific implication. First, as he writes in the *Institutes of the Christian Religion*, there is *"a universal call* by which God, through the external preaching of the word, invites all...alike even those for whom he designs the call to be a savour of death, and the ground of a severer condemnation."[10] God's universal call awakens the elect and condemns the non-elect. Second, there is what Calvin called *"a special call* which, for the most part, God bestows on believers only, when by the internal illumination of the Spirit he causes the word preached to take deep root in their hearts." For Calvin, the "special call," dare we say vocation, includes the illumination of the Spirit fostering a new understanding of who we are. Then, just to let us know who is in charge (God, not Calvin),

[8] Thomas Merton, *Raids on the Unspeakable* (Tunbridge Wells UK: Burns & Oates, reprinted 1988) 126–27.

[9] Ibid., 135.

[10] John Calvin, *Institutes of the Christian Religion* vol. 2 (Edinburgh UK: T. & T. Clark, 1863) 247.

Calvin adds: "Sometimes, however, [God] communicates it also to those whom he enlightens only for a time, and whom afterwards, in just punishment for their ingratitude, he abandons and smites with greater blindness."[11] I'm glad we only have to give letter grades!

Seventeenth-century Baptists and Quakers added another dimension to this idea of vocation, anticipating modernity and moving radically beyond the medievalism of Luther and Calvin to what I would call the egalitarianism of vocation. For Baptists, faith in Christ was the doorway to vocation; it was God's ultimate calling that broke down barriers of economics, class, education, and clergy/laity distinctions. (Many were late to discover its radical equality of race, however.) Many early Baptists symbolized that equality by laying hands on twice, once to the newly baptized and a second time for those set aside for "peculiar" service in the ministry of the word. For those Baptists every Christian received a special calling at baptism, and the coming of the Spirit symbolized by the laying on of hands equally. I think their understanding of vocation was inseparable from their concern for conscience, and that leads me to the academic setting. As a Baptist, I don't trust institutions. Indeed, I learned in Louisville that if you trust academic institutions you will probably be terribly disappointed, if not altogether done in by them. I do not expect such institutions to respond to life and learning in ways that are always compatible with my identity as professor and person of faith (although I hope for that). But what I expect is VOICE, the freedom to speak out of conscience when necessary, and a reasonably safe environment in which to live out of conscience as best I can. Thus voice, freedom, conscience, and CIVILITY are all bound up together in every academic context.

For Quakers, the inner light was the great equalizer, only to be recognized as the source of everyone's vocation to serve. The "light within" was the source of everyone's identity/vocation. Men and women, overtaken by the Spirit, could proclaim the gospel and lead the community of faith. In the late twentieth and early twenty-first century, ideas fostered by liberation theology, multiculturalism, evangelicalism, feminism, and sexuality studies have offered other "foundations" for one's sense of vocation.

---

[11] Ibid.

Right now, I think we Protestants remain confused about the nature and formation of vocation. I think we want to talk about vocation using the language of Calvin but with the spirituality of Merton, drawn to the mystical body of Christ, but attempting to organize it to "beat the devil" all in a world where new theologies, exploding technologies, and unbridled religious disaffection challenge our culture privilege and our ability to explain ourselves in the public square.

The dilemma is nothing new; it has simply become more intensified. Richard T. Hughes asks the central question: "How is it possible for Christian institutions of higher learning to develop into academic institutions of the first order and, at the same time, to nurture in creative ways the faith commitments that called these institutions into existence in the first place? More than this, how is it possible for Christian Colleges and universities to weave first-class academic programs from the very fabric of their faith commitments?"[12] Given these historic options perhaps we can claim the following ideas together.

First, let us say that the idea of vocation has multiple interpretations, varied choices, and differing approaches. At its best, each school should offer, cultivate, a context, a "safe place," for exploration of those diverse—sometimes divisive—approaches to the nature of vocation itself.

Second, perhaps vocational formation is an implicit, if not explicit, part of higher education from a Christian perspective. Research, writing, class discussion/debate facilitate, as Buechner says, the search for a self to be, for selves to love, and for work to do.

Third, (and this is my bias, I suppose) let us say that vocation is at its best when it has an edge to it or at the very least strengthens a sense of self, one's identity in the world, BEFORE the inevitable tragedy or conflict strikes. I would suggest that one Baptist way (no doubt among many) for responding to the changing nature of campus life would be a reassertion of those early Baptist ideals of dissent, conscience and believers' church. That is, Baptists should be at the forefront of the quest for "voice" on college and university campus, not as a tepid, grudging response to nebulous political correctness, but because "voice" is endemic to the nature of Baptist identity, perhaps even its most profound distinctive. Baptist schools might lead the way in drawing on

---

[12] Richard T. Hughes and William B. Adrian, eds., *Models for Christian Higher Education* (Grand Rapids MI: Eerdmans, 1997) 1.

this heritage to encourage and facilitate dialogue, dissent, and cultivation of conscience, not because that is the secular wave of the future, but because their tradition recognized the value of these ideals earlier than any other modern Protestant communion.

Journalist, secularist, bohemian, Dorothy Day's sense of vocation began, in a way, with the first pangs of morning sickness and the realization that she and her longtime lover Forster Batterham, were to have a baby. Here is how she described it:

> When I wrote the story of my conversion twelve years ago, I left out all my sins but told of all the things which brought me to god, all the beautiful things, all the remembrances of God that had haunted me, pursued me over the years so that when my daughter was born, in grateful joy I turned to God and became a Catholic. I could worship, adore, praise and thank him in the company of others. It is difficult to do that without a ritual, without a body with which to love and move, love and praise. I found faith, I became a member of the Mystical Body of Christ.[13]

Her lover, a committed agnostic and anarchist, could not endure her decision and left her and their child. Day raised their daughter, Tamara, and founded the Catholic Worker Movement, one of the most important social movements of the twentieth century. Her sense of vocation led her to the edginess of a radical involvement with the poor in an organization that endures to this day. "All my life I have been haunted by God," Day said.[14] You too?

---

[13] Dorothy Day, *The Long Loneliness: An Autobiography* (San Francisco: Harper & Row, 1952) 10.

[14] Ibid., 11.

Part II: SERMONS: A WITNESS OF THE CHURCH

# Abraham and Sarah: The Risk of Faith

## Genesis 12:1–9

The sun had not yet risen when they started out across the desert. "I hope we got everything," the woman remarked. "We took what we could," the man replied. "Which way are we headed,"? Sarai asked quietly. "That way," her husband answered, pointing to the distant horizon, "at least for today."

Risky business, faith—at least the way Abram, AKA Abraham, experienced it. Abram was a nomad, roaming desert regions following sheep and goats, moving from oasis to oasis for water, grace and a bit of shade in the burning Middle Eastern heat. His father, Terah, was a nomad, too, and Genesis chapter 11:31 says: "Terah took his son Abram, his grandson Lot the son of Haran, and his daughter in law Sarai, Abram's wife, and they set out from Ur of the Chaldees for Canaan. But when they reached Harran, they settled there." Ur of the Chaldeans is out in the Arabian Desert—Iraq, actually—where it can reach upwards of 113 degrees. (Ironically, Ur of the Chaldeans has significance for families in our country three thousand years after Abraham and his family lived there.) A friend of mine who has served in Iraq says he has been to Ur and knows exactly why Abraham got out of there. It is hot as blazes; a pretty bleak desert place, even now.

So they headed for Canaan but stopped at Harran, about half way from where they were supposed to be, and, the text says, "they settled there." Like most nomadic desert tribes, they were a pretty tight-knit clan. It must have been a decent enough place, and Abram seemed all tucked in until there came a word from "the Lord":

> Leave your own country, your kin, and your father's house, and go to a country that I will show you. I shall make you into a great nation. I shall bless you and make your name so great that it will be used in blessings. (Gen. 12:3)

And Abram/Abraham goes. He just picks up and goes. On one level, for people like us with our interstates, and U-Haul trucks, and cell phones, that doesn't seem too difficult. But consider this: Abram has to "leave his father's house," not an easy thing to do in this tribal culture where social security meant you lived with your parents, aunts, and uncles and took care of them to the end. In the tent, in the desert, every home is an assisted living home, where young and old bump up against each other day to day and year to year.

Truth to tell, Abram does not have much knowledge of the "Lord" who is speaking to him. Who is this desert deity, just another nomadic god among multitudes of deities worshiped by various tribes out in the backside of the desert? What was it about this God that got his attention?

This encounter between God and Abram in Genesis 12 is really the beginning of the Jewish people and their understanding of monotheism, the one God who is distinct from all the many. So Abram's great decision is not whether he should leave home or obey the God who is telling him to go. In that, we are not much different from Abraham and his ancient story. Before you pull up stakes then or NOW, you'd better decide whose God is telling you to do so, if God is speaking to you at all. Believing in God, listening to God's "voice" is as risky now as it was then.

If Abram struggled over all this, the text doesn't say. It says he just went, but, like a good nomad, he did not go alone. I love how Genesis describes their departure: He took his wife Sarai, his nephew Lot, all their possessions, and "the dependents they had acquired in Harran, and they departed for Canaan" (Gen. 12:5). "Dependents" sound like an IRS audit, doesn't it? God told him to go and he took the dependents he had acquired with him.

Some people call it wanderlust, I suppose, an obsession to see what is on the other side of the next hill or sand dune. But what seemed just another nomadic adventure became a historic risk of faith for Abraham, Sarah, the Jews, the Arabs, and the rest of us. Draw a line today from this pulpit through seventeenth-century Baptists, to Martin Luther, to Augustine of Hippo, to Jesus of Nazareth, to John the Baptizer, to David, and Moses, and Abraham, and we discover that we were all among Abraham's dependents in some sense or another, loading up to head for the land of Canaan. (And, by the way, don't forget that your local imam can draw a line from Mohammed to Ishmael to Abraham as directly as we can!)

While you are calculating all that, also remember that the writer of Hebrews says: "By faith Abraham settled as an alien in the land promised him, living in tents, as did Isaac and Jacob, who were heirs to the same promise. For he looked forward to the city with firm foundations, whose architect and builder is God" (Heb. 11:9–10 REB).

The way the Bible tells it, this was no mere whim. If Abraham did this impulsively, he also did it by faith. Yet such faith is a risk, pure and simple. O, we say, it was not so risky; Abraham knew that God would take care of him. After all, God sweetened the pot by telling him up front: "I will make you a great nation. I will bless you and make your name so great that is shall be used as a blessing. Your descendants will be more than the sands of the seashore and all families on earth will pray to be blessed as you are blessed." In fact, he was to be so famous that a whole nation will call you "father."

Sounds wonderful, doesn't it? No risk here, just a promise from GOD. But remember, they don't know anything about this GOD, have no history with this God till now. And the promise is made out in the desert to a man and a woman who, after years of trying, can't make one baby, let alone a whole "sands of the seashore" crowd of children. Even before they left Ur of the Chaldeans, Genesis labeled Abram's spouse: "Sarai was barren; she had no child" (Gen. 11:30). And, if you were female in that desert society then and now, "barren" was the worst name they could pin on you.

Abram and Sarai had no more assurance that things would work out than we do, maybe less, because we at least know something of the history of God's activity in the world. They were starting this monotheism thing from scratch. With this barren woman, the odds on producing a great nation were about the same as if a truck pulled up in front of your house with a Publisher's Clearinghouse check for a million dollars, or you got the winning numbers off of a ticket you picked at the BP station last night. Home was a sure thing. Leaving home, even by faith, was not. It was the risk of faith.

Whether you go or stay, whether you believe in God at home or on the interstate, faith is still a risk. Abraham is not the only example, is he? Moses hears God in a burning bush in "the backside of the desert" and is told to speak to Pharaoh: "Let my people go," and he almost laughs in God's face: "I have a speech impediment," he blurts back, "and I can't possibly risk it." (Actually, he says, "I am a man of uncircumcised lips," but we won't talk like that on a Sunday morning.)

In short, Moses asks what Abraham asks: "Why me?" But he risks it for God's sake, and the children of Israel are set free again. Simon Peter and some of his fishing buddies hear the words of Jesus of Nazareth: "Follow me and I will teach you to cast your nets for people." And they follow him, never knowing for a moment where it will take them, and if they had known they would probably never have stayed with their friends at the bait shop.

People still do it, don't they—decide to risk something of themselves in response to what they think is God's mandate for them? Almost every week of my life for a period of time a student would settle onto the couch in my divinity school office and say something like: "I'm not sure why I'm here, but I have to talk to someone about this ministry thing." Or: "I'm not sure at all what I will do, but I have to DO THIS!" Some have known they had to do it from the beginning—care for persons who are hurting, preach the gospel, fight for Justice in Jesus' name, become missionaries, chaplains, social workers, pastors, disturbers of the civil and religious peace. But some, most, haven't a clue. They are terrified that they might wind up here, killing a perfectly good Sunday morning in some pulpit or the other.

In story after story, these folks, some out of college, some middle aged, some even more "mature" leave something behind and follow, and I am humbled and honored to get to hear the story and talk with them, whether they come to WFU or not. Watching them move toward ministry, become helpers in new and creative ways is one of the greatest experiences in the world.

Risky business: faith, growth, maturity, birth, and rebirth. Faith is knowing or hoping you know when to go and when to stay, when to watch and pray, and when to launch out, in doing what you have to do, going where you have to go, following the voice of God that will not let you rest until you do it.

Abram, like all of us, looked for a place—a place to discover God, to face life, to raise a family, to put down roots. He looked for a place to belong, a place to believe. In faith he risked the possibility that in leaving one place he might never find another. In fact, if you read on in the text it says that no sooner had they gotten to Canaan than there was a famine and they were forced to flee to Egypt. "Thanks, God, I'm certainly glad I did what you told me," Abram might have said. "I was willing to go to Texas, but the famine came and I had to go to Oklahoma! Now that is just too much faith!"

But he did find a place, they did have a child (note that risk, in one of the Bible's most human and hilarious passages), and a nation was born, still risking its identity in modern Israel, as amazing and as controversial as when Abraham showed up on the land.

Abraham's search for a place is important for all of us, since place is not merely geographical, it is spiritual and personal. Everybody searches for a place where they belong, where they feel at home, and where they think they might find God. Some people simply find it more easily than others. Why do some people find their place almost from the beginning and never turn aside from that original vision? Faith comes to them through family, church, experience as real in gentle nurture as in turmoil and chaos. They hear, know, and follow, and the place of faith holds across the years. Others fight with it, fight with God, fight with their place, and fight with themselves almost from the beginning. Getting somewhere, anywhere, is always a struggle for some of us.

But what happens when the place of faith changes and you can't stay there any longer? When you lose your place, do you lose your faith? What do you do when the religion of your childhood won't hold any more, not because it isn't good, but because it isn't enough? Suddenly you realize that the most wonderful place in the world is hell on earth when you cannot resolve the turmoil in your own heart. Or when turmoil from outside descends on you, what then? When the place is a maternity ward and a doctor with antiseptic indifference says: "Sorry, we will have to keep your baby for a week or so, there are some complications," and the place of joy turns into the place of terror. What then? Life takes a turn and the place of blessing is something unexpected—can you still risk faith?

The word of God that came to Abraham and Sarah comes to us: "The just shall live by faith" (Rom. 1:17). No place guarantees God's presence, but no place is immune from it either. We, like Abraham and Sarah, discover that whatever the place, God has been there all along. The Gospel that both Abraham and St. Paul brings to us is beyond who you are, beyond what you have done, beyond where you come from or where you are going. There is a place for you. So we live by that risky faith that God is present with us even when we do not know which road to take or even have a clear map of where we are going. Where faith is concerned we are called to grow, and we can't stay any place forever.

Think of all the places where faith of God's people has bubbled up: On the way to Canaan, on the way out of Egypt, on the sea of Galilee, at the place of the skull, in the sick room, the classroom, or the upper room. Faith is not always sure and certain, sometimes it is risky and ragged, but it is out there in front of us, calling us to be better than we thought we could ever be on a journey. Think it's worth the risk?

# Beset By Weakness

## Hebrews 5:1–10; Mark 10 32–45

St. Peter denied Jesus three times; St. Augustine, the early church's great theologian, had a mistress for fifteen years. He writes about her but never bothers to tell us her name. St. Francis of Assisi displayed behavior that might now be considered a kind of psychic hysteria; and St. Teresa of Avila would probably be highly sedated or even institutionalized today. Martin Luther was a raving anti-Semite; John Calvin approved the burning of Michael Servetus because of his view of the Trinity; John Wesley had terrible relationships with women, and his estranged wife was dead a week before he learned of it. Jonathan Edwards, that sinner in the hands of an angry God, was fired from his first church and never had another. Harry Emerson Fosdick the liberal pastor of Riverside Church, New York, had an emotional collapse early in his ministry; J. Frank Norris fundamentalist pastor of First Baptist church, Fort Worth, shot and killed an unarmed man; the Apostle Paul testified to a mysterious "thorn in the flesh" that even heartfelt prayer could not take away, and some of us aren't looking all that great. "I am weak but thou art strong," the Gospel hymn declares. "Jesus keep me from all wrong." We are weak, aren't we? Indeed, if original sin haunts humanity so does original weakness. We all have it.

The writer of Hebrews captures that condition in a powerful image that leaps out at us from today's New Testament text. The passage is yet another attempt by yet another biblical writer to explain what it is that made a Palestinian Jew the savior of the world, to reach back into the history of Israel for a metaphor, a single clue as to why Jesus' death and resurrection has anything to do with us. "He's like a high priest," the writer says, "one taken directly from the people and "appointed their representative by God," in order to offer "gifts and sacrifices" (in the temple) to help them deal with that most basic human traits: sin. In describing the nature of the high priestly office, preparing to compare it to the work of Jesus Christ, Hebrews offers a great line that I don't think I had ever really heard before: (I confess to you that all the conversation here about high priests and the strange figure of Melchizedek I've tended to leave to my colleagues in biblical studies and to Premillennialist preachers on cable television.) But lectionary preaching forced me to revisit these ancient ideas, and I found them overwhelming. I'm particularly taken with the way the Revised English Bible translates this passage. It suggests that the high priest, called out from the people, "is able to bear patiently with the ignorant and erring, since *he too is beset by weakness.* (Heb. 5:2 REB).

And there it is again, one small biblical idea that captures our common condition. The text says out loud what our inner lives all ready know: We are a race at times ignorant, erring, and beset by weakness. It's how we are. That weakness is complex, sure enough. Sometimes our weakness is evident in willful action with moral implications. We fall victim to choices we should never have made and that carry us into places we wish we'd never gone. St. Paul describes that weakness as present deep within himself when he writes: "The good which I want to do, I fail to do. I discover this principle, then: that when I want to do the right, only the wrong is within my reach." And he asks: "O wretched one that I am, who will deliver me from this body of death?" (Rom. 7:19, 21) Some of us spend too much of our lives playing to our weaknesses. Simple weakness can turn to obsession all too easily. For a moment, let every one of us fill in this blank: "I have a real weakness for _____." And then let's ask ourselves where has that weakness taken us physically, mentally, spiritually, or communally? Where and when have our acknowledged or unacknowledged weaknesses led us into actions the writer of Hebrews describes with that singularly dark and dangerous word, sin, a word has lost its meaning in part because we use it so much in church but understand it so little. Beset by weakness, we slide right into sin.

Those saintly brothers, James and John, apparently had quite a weakness for prestige and privilege, at one point convincing even their mama to ask Jesus to give them special treatment. In today's Gospel text they ask Jesus a question that reveals how "ignorant and erring" they are even after weeks of living in continuous proximity to the Word of God made flesh. They can't seem to shake the idea that all of Jesus' words about the KINGDOM OF GOD must apply to an earthly, religio-political kingdom that replaces or at least parallels the Roman Empire being acted out in their midst. So they ask this little weasel-question behind the backs of their apostolic fraternity brothers: "Master, we would like for you to do us a favor." A favor? Are they kidding? Sure, they'd already met lots of people who asked for favors from Jesus—heal my son, heal my daughter, heal my mother-in-law (Peter asked that), heal my friend, heal me. But here they are asking him for a place in the Kingdom, and a special place at that. Maybe they thought, "Jesus, you cave in to every Tom, Dick, and Mary Magdalene that asks you for something. Surely you can do a little favor for us! We've given up more than any of the others so can we have the sky-box seats in your kingdom, the one closest to you and the big buffet table?"

Their weakness for prestige and privilege forced Jesus to remind them what it seems they would not hear: This kingdom he proclaims is about difficulty and death. The "cup" you have to drink is laced with danger so don't gulp it down too quickly. And then he adds in one of those verses that Calvinists love and the rest of us wrestle with in free-will-friendly Sunday School classes, angry blogs, or late-night-religion-major dormitory discussions: "These seats are not mine to give. They have already been assigned!" Let's not go there today, ok?

James and John are fascinating symbols of that most basic human weakness: the obsession with self that seeks prestige and privilege, promotes hierarchy, and courts special favors from the Divine. Indeed, one of the greatest dangers, shall we just say sins, of religious folk in our time and place—American Protestant Christianity—is this idea that grace is an entitlement that forces God to act in whatever way we ask, whenever and whatever we want. It is a terrible weakness of religious folk in our time.

But sometimes the weakness of the human condition is not of our choosing. It is part of our context. Some people aren't weakened by sin; they are weakened by life. Annie Dillard runs a dramatic list when she writes: "A hundred million of us are children who live on the streets.... three percent of us are mentally retarded; Twenty-three million of us are refugees.... two thousand of us a day commit suicide; ...thirty million...not yet age five die each year."[1] Many of us grow us as "tender plants," don't we? All of us feel like "roots out of dry ground" at some point.

---

[1] Annie Dillard, *For the Time Being* (New York: Alfred A. Knopf, 1999) 130.

Amid apostolic weakness, ambition and indignation Jesus changes the entire subject. The way he tells it, servanthood is both a sign of weakness—we make ourselves vulnerable by serving others—and a way out of weakness—we overcome the sins and obsessions that haunt us by giving ourselves away for others. Jesus himself washed feet, for God's sake!

Years ago I was the last interim pastor at the Twenty-third and Broadway Baptist Church in Louisville, Kentucky. It was a venerable, old, inner-city congregation that had flourished for generations and was the first inter-racial church I had ever served. But the neighborhood was changing, and people of multiple races were moving out. By the time I got there, the church was on its last legs, knowing they would call a full-time pastor who would preside over the church's closing. And what a church they were, caring, affirming, trying to minister to their vanishing community to the bitter end. So they elected Mrs. Jones a deacon. She was in her eighties, had Parkinson's, and had been a member of that church for decades. In the last years of her life, and theirs, they elected Mrs. Jones a deacon. And each first Sunday of the month when we had communion she would come forward with the deacons and gather at Christ's table. Her hands shook so badly from Parkinson's that she could not carry the trays, but she came to the table and would walk alongside another deacon as he or she served bread and the cup. I shall never forget the image of that woman shuffling, shaking, caring down the aisle of a slowly disintegrating but gospel-filled congregation, signs of inescapable weakness for church and individual, still serving, still caring, still loving—strength made perfect in weakness to the inevitable Gospel end. Amen.

# Breathing the Spirit:
# A Hesitant Faith

## John 20:19-29

They all doubted—you know, the APOSTLES—those who were there at the end of the beginning. The women were an exception, so the story goes, especially the "ones who came with him from Galilee," who lingered at the cross to the bitter end and discovered the empty tomb as Easter morning broke. As usual, the men didn't believe them (nothing ever changes).

Luke tells it like this: "The women were Mary of Magdala, Joanna, and Mary the mother of James and they, with the other women told these things to the apostles." Nonetheless, apostolic doubt prevailed, as the text continues: "But the story appeared to them to be NONESENSE, and they would not believe them." NONSENSE? Before you get too deep into this so-called Good News, you've got to deal with the "nonsense" of Jesus and his story, of Jesus and his love. They all doubted, Thomas just said it out loud.

Thomas wasn't there when Jesus finally showed himself to an apostolic community cowering in fear behind closed doors. "He breathed on them," today's text says, and told them, "receive the Holy Spirit." "He breathed on them," then offered a word that is both promise and warning: "As the Father has sent me, so I send you."

But Thomas wasn't there. Thomas didn't suck in a single breath of the spirit. In fact, Thomas would have none of it, unless, as he said, "I put my finger into the place where the nails were..." Short of that, he declared: "I will not believe it."

Perhaps Thomas is less an apostolic doubter, than a hesitant realist. His action in today's New Testament lesson has the tone of realism about it. After all, he knew that Jesus of Nazareth was "crucified, dead and buried," and dead meant dead, a sorrowful but inevitable reality, then and now. Luke says that even those who had seen Jesus "thought they were seeing a ghost," and continued to be "startled and terrified." No doubt Thomas had heard the stories, talked to the women. But he says out loud what many of the others were thinking. Luke's gospel says it straight up for them and us: "They were still incredulous, still astounded, for it seemed too good to be true" (Luke 24:41).

Like many of us, Thomas wants to believe. It isn't that he doubts, he's just hesitant, precisely because it seems *too good to be true.* Thomas is a realist. He simply wants to know that this "women's story"—beyond belief—is even remotely possible. So he declares: "Unless I touch the wounds in his hands, feet and side, I WILL NOT believe." His is at best a hesitant faith.

But this story isn't just about touching wounds, flesh, and blood. There is something else going on here, something in the text that ought to make us all hesitant when we reflect on it. Jesus breathes the spirit into them, with the affirmative warning: "As the Father sent me, so I sent you." "Where I go," he says, breathlessly, "you must go."

And surely they understood him standing there with pierced hands and feet. Where had Jesus been? To the cross, of course. So here is the warning to Thomas and to all of us: don't gulp down the Spirit too readily. It could get you into lots of trouble. Perhaps Thomas knows exactly where this Jesus way will take him. He wants to be sure that Jesus is present, is risen, and is ready to be with him for the long haul. The Spirit blows where it will; in fact the Holy Spirit is not an entitlement; it is a dangerous breath to take.

So in the "season" of Pentecost, here is a word for us to consider today about the spirit and the future. First, the church in general, and this church in particular, is a community in which persons like ourselves breathe the Spirit in life transforming ways. Second, before we breathe in the Spirit too quickly, let us consider where it may take us. Let's start with the scary part first: Thomas's demand—to encounter and touch the risen Christ—captures one of the great dilemmas of Christian spirituality, the link between dangerous faith and hesitant realism. Is the Jesus story too good to be true, or is it "reality," a verifiable reality that is worth our trust, our energy, and our very lives? That became a great dilemma for many of us the minute the women brought news of the empty tomb reached those "incredulous" apostles. Honest Thomas, realistic Thomas, hesitant Thomas asks the questions for the rest of us then and now.

And Jesus acquiesces. He reveals himself to Thomas, who touches him and believes, confessing dramatically: "My Lord and my God." But then Jesus gives a two-sentence sermon that stretches from that upper room to this very day. The King James Bible translates it with poetic power as Jesus says: "Because thou hast seen me, thou hast believed: blessed are they that have not seen, and YET have believed" (John 20:29).

That's us, right, the ones who have not seen yet believe, or want to? So we go to great lengths to prove it true. We concoct so many methods for softening Jesus' terrifying calling or concretizing faith as substantially as possible. Some people have touched Jesus' hands and sides by making the Bible inerrant—without error in every subject it discusses—making the design intelligent, the rules clear, and the doctrines non-negotiable. With an inerrant text we can touch Christ's nail-pierced hands, believe, and never hesitate again. Others link themselves directly with the apostles, an unbroken succession passed on from Jesus and Thomas. Still others touch Jesus' wounds through restoring the practices of the early church—tongues, miracles, healing—rising up from the day of Pentecost with assurance of God's continuing presence in the world. Still others point to the unending tradition of religious experience in conversion and mystical encounter. Each has its own validity and assurance for those who stand inside the varied traditions of the Christian church itself. Blessed are they. Some go farther still, promising miracles as an entitlement, there for the taking for all who have the right access code to the divine bank account—modern indulgence sellers no less problematic than those challenged by Martin Luther five hundred years ago.

Jesus' words extend beyond all our traditions, reasonable or irrelevant as they may be. They challenge the easy faith of false promises made in the name of God. His remarks to Thomas call us to go beyond our creaturely attempts to verify it all, alleviating all hesitancy. But faith at its heart moves beyond reason to risk; it calls us to accept the danger of not seeing everything before we cast ourselves on the risen Christ. Jesus accepts Thomas' hesitant quest for proof, but he goes beyond it to insist that in reality there is nothing Thomas or the rest of us can do to prove Jesus' words and no way to make them safe enough to avoid radical faith. "Blessed are those who believe even when they do not see." Amid all the proofs and proof texts, sooner or later we are forced to confront the astonishing and dangerous news of Jesus' teaching, his death, and resurrection, and his calling to get on down the road with him.

Perhaps Thomas' request is not simply a way of proving faith, it is a way of possessing Jesus, owning him a bit, and making his message more manageable. But, sooner or later, Jesus leaps over the boundaries we set for him. He is, as Gary Wills wrote recently, the perpetual revolutionary whose message resists systematic attempts to control it and set it inside boundaries of our own creation.[1]

I wonder if any of the terrified disciples in the upper room, still a long way from Pentecost, remembered the wedding at Cana in Galilee where Jesus turned water into wine. All the apostles were there, John's gospel says, along with Jesus' mother, who urged Jesus to save the party by providing a great Merlot (or something like that). And he does—180 gallons of wine so superb that the caterer says: "Usually we serve the best wine first and wait until the guests are a little buzzed (its in the text), but you have saved the best until last." You see, at Cana they breathed in spirits *and* the Spirit.

And the story concludes with this kingdom of God observation: "This was the first of Jesus' signs that revealed his glory and led his disciples to believe in him." How easy it was in those early days to follow the hospitable messiah who provided refreshments at parties. What a great upper room memory, so far from hope.

I've breathed the Spirit a time or two, when it appeared that God had saved the best until last, when the Spirit fell and I knew it beyond a reasonable doubt.

Two very deep memories relate to baptism—an event fraught with celebration and danger all at once. I remember the day when, as an interim pastor at a big liturgically serious Louisville church, I entered their baptistery with a man named Bob with whom I'd discussed matters of faith for months. We talked of life and death, faith and hope, but not until he entered the water with me did I realize that he was more than six feet tall and weighed "substantially," shall we say. And I knew it was over when I looked out into the congregation and saw my wife put her head in her hands. But down he went with the name of God spoken over him and down I went, too, with water pouring into the hip boots. Somehow, grace mostly with a modicum of adrenalin, we got back up to a congregation that broke into spontaneous applause. They thought

---

[1] Gary Wills, *What Jesus Meant* (New York: Penguin, 2007).

they'd lost both of us that morning. We all breathed the Spirit (and a sigh of relief).

But there was another baptism, thirteen years later, in the same baptistery just before we moved from Louisville. On Christmas Eve 1991, our daughter Stephanie, a person with special needs, then sixteen, entered the baptistery of that church with her pastor, Stephen Shoemaker, who, by the way, accepted her with the best of pastoral responses when she requested it. Her mother and I thought we'd deal with logistics up in the baptistery, but we were promptly dismissed by Mildred Birch, one of the "mothers of the church." "You need to be out there where you can see this wonderful event," she declared. "I'll take care of Stephanie." So into the water Stephanie went, "Confess your faith," Pastor Shoemaker said. "Jesus is Lord," our daughter replied, and under she went, in the name of Father, Son, and Holy Spirit. And then out she went, with Mildred Birch standing on the edge of the baptistery, enfolding her in a towel, and welcoming her new Christian sister home.

To this very day, the breath of the Spirit lingers in Stephanie Leonard, breathed on her through Mildred Birch and a loving congregation. And when my faith is as hesitant as Thomas's, I remember that moment and, like the folks at Cana, I get a little buzzed with the Spirit. And the best was saved till last.

Let's say it one more time: We are all special needs children, you and I, in some it is just more public than in others. At its best Christ's church must keep breathing out the Spirit on human beings, every one of them with special needs. "Blessed are they who do not see, but still believe."

"He breathed on them," the Bible says, and told them to receive the Spirit. Two thousand years later, let's claim the Spirit one more time, carrying us through a sometimes checkered past, calling us to a hopeful future, and drawing us together as a caring, sometimes broken, community.

Perhaps the Spirit will find us, even if it does seem too good to be true.

Yes, *by God,* it just might be blowing in on us right now.

Take a deep, deep breath.

# Dancing with the Prophetic

## Mark 6:14–29

John the Baptist scares me, always has. He's so, well, so prophetic, a formidable presence from the beginning, kicking to high heaven in his mama's belly when the Virgin Mary came to visit, celebrating the embryonic presence of cousin Jesus before either of them entered the world. Indeed, John's mother Elizabeth says to Jesus' mother Mary: "I tell you, when your greeting sounded in my ears, the baby in my womb leapt for joy (Luke 1:44). Apparently, John was prophetic even in utero.

He comes of age in the Judean desert, keeping company perhaps with the crowd at Qumran who anticipated the pending "Day of the Lord" when God would finally take charge of the corrupt Roman world. John storms out of the wilderness wearing a camel's hair tunic and feasting on a happy meal of locusts and wild honey—a high protein diet of desert s'mores. "Repent," he says, for the kingdom of heaven is headed your way. God's messenger is coming, and when he gets here it will not be pretty. "He will gather the wheat into his granary, but the chaff he will burn on a fire that can never be put out" (Matt. 3:12). All that eternal fire talk seems to have gotten their attention since Matthew says that the crowds "flocked to him," "from Jerusalem, Judea, and the Jordan Valley, and were baptized by him in the river Jordan, confessing their SINS" (Matt. 3:5–6).

As a child, I was fascinated—and terrified—by John. He seemed lean and mean, direct and outspoken, like most of the Texas evangelists I grew up hearing, a revival preacher in camel skin. In fact, you had to like John. He was a Baptist, after all. There is that great story of the two frontier preachers arguing over whose church was the most biblically correct. The Baptist preacher, feeling himself bested, finally exclaimed: "Well, they didn't call him John the Presbyterian, did they?"

John scares me still. In fact, two thousand years later, today's gospel story confronts us with daunting religious questions: What in the world is the "prophetic," and what does it have to do with us? Who is a prophet and who is not, and how do you know the difference? When do prophets speak for God, and when are they just plain crazy?

Today's story illustrates the dilemma. Herod Antipas knows he needs to rid himself of the meddlesome Baptist whose message could foment rebellion, but he is hesitant to offend the rabble by killing so popular a preacher. Indeed, Josephus, the first-century Jewish historian, says that after hearing John's preaching, Herod feared that the "Eloquence that had so great an effect on humanity might lead to some form of sedition."[1] Prophets fascinate us, even as we fear them. Herod needs a reason to do John in. Enter Salome and her mother Herodias, two women who are provocative and pathetic all at once, females exploiting and exploited by power, offering Herod a convenient pretext for silencing the cranky prophet. (In fact, we could have talked at length about the child abuse evident in this text.)

It's an earthy book, the Bible. John, like many prophets, does not hesitate to criticize the actions of the privileged class, those ruling families who think they, unlike the rest of us, are ethically immune (thank God that does not happen today!). "You have no right to take your brother's wife," he says to Antipas, upbraiding Herod and infuriating "the other woman," Herodias, and setting himself on a collision course with culture and power. The beautiful Salome dances, and Herod, the dirty old man, promises her anything. His offended spouse manipulates the occasion, and Herod gets the perfect ruse for doing what he wanted to do anyway. "I promised her anything she wanted!" John is beheaded, and that should have ended the matter. But in the pitch-dark hours of the morning, Herod frets that the Baptist might come back to haunt him, literally.

What a story, the stuff of multiple novels, plays, movies, and of course, sermons. One southern preacher was alleged to have preached a sermon that used this text for a moral warning to youth entitled, "The Baptist Preacher who lost his head at a Dance."[2]

Today, let us say that the dance in this story is not primarily Salome's, it is Herod's and ours as well. Indeed, dancing with the prophetic is something that Herod can neither ignore nor endure. The

---

[1] John Dominic Crossan, *God & Empire: Jesus Against Rome, Then and Now* (San Francisco: HarperOne, 2007) 112.

[2] This anecdotal account attributes the sermon to either J. Frank Norris of Texas or John R. Rice of Tennessee, both prominent twentieth-century fundamentalist Baptists.

text says that Herod "liked to listen to John, although what he heard left him greatly disturbed." He dances with the prophetic, but it makes him miserable. He is intrigued by John's rhetoric, even as he detests its message.

At best, prophets like John help us get our bearings in the world. They throw cold water and hard sayings in our faces and force us to take stock of our lives and the culture around us. At worst, dancing with the prophetic may mean that we find an excuse to silence the messenger and the message, ignoring it or manipulating our way out of responding to the warnings. As enchanted as Herod may have been with John, it is clear that he knew John had to be silenced. Perhaps Salome and her dance were just an excuse. Herod blames the woman, refusing to take responsibility for his decision. Indeed, the prophetic landscape is covered with the bodies of the dead, some of whom, though silenced by death, speak yet. The Baptizer, along with Peter and Paul, Polycarp, Perpetua, and Felicitas in the early church, and later John Hus, Michael Servetus, and Balthazar Hubmaier, Quaker Mary Dyer, Lutheran Dietrich Bonhoeffer, and Martin Luther King—each offered a prophetic word and were silenced, often with the religious community as accessory.

Defining the prophetic is no easy matter. Some prophets "fore-tell"; they look into the future and tell the rest of us what lies ahead, usually with a warning of the wrath that is to come. Jeremiah foretells the word of God to Judah: "You will lose possession of the land which I gave you. I shall make you serve your enemies in a land you do not know; for the fire of my anger is kindled by you, and it will burn forever" (Jer. 17:4). And it happened.

John Woolman, the colonial Quaker, travels throughout the South urging Quakers to free their slaves a hundred years before emancipation, warning that a refusal to do so would result in a broken nation. And it happened. Like John, some prophets foretell: God is going to clear the decks; society is in trouble and it is going to get rough before it gets better. Best to get your hearts right.

But prophets also "forth-tell" the Word of God. They say what they see and challenge the status quo for religious and non-religious alike. Amos speaks the "word of the Lord," declaring: "For I know how many are your crimes, how monstrous your sins: you bully the innocent, extort ransoms, and in court push the destitute out of the way. In such a time, therefore, it is prudent to stay quiet, for it is an evil time" (Amos 5:12–13). "You are the children of vipers," John the Baptizer says to the religious crowd of his day. "Prove your repentance by the fruit that you bear" (Matt. 3:7–8).

At other times, the prophetic is a word of hope in a time of trouble, when things are so bad that the only way out is for God to do a new thing. Some prophets promise that sooner or later God will set things right. In today's text from the Hebrew Bible, David dances toward the prophetic, not away from it, and celebrates the fulfillment of God's own prophetic word to Abraham, Isaac, Jacob, and Moses. He follows the Ark of the Covenant into Jerusalem; "nekked" as the Appalachian preachers often say, dancing his heart out in joy, awe, and wonder in the fulfilling presence of Israel's God. Sometimes the good things the prophet promises do occur and, like David, we can't contain our joy at living to see it.

And wasn't Rosa Parks acting prophetically when she refused to move to the back of the Cleveland Avenue bus in Montgomery, Alabama, on that December day more than half a century ago? That quiet, but determined response to one of the great signs of American racism was a prophetic indictment of Jim Crow culture. But it was also the promise that things could be changed when many people, black and white, thought they never could. We're not home yet where racism is concerned, but we are a long, long way from Montgomery, Alabama, of 1955. I saw that recently in a *New York Times* photo of the bare feet of one of the Obama daughters in the back of the presidential limo on her way to meet the Pope in Rome. From the back of the bus to the presidential limo. Rosa Parks was a prophet for all of us. Jim Crow is dead; let's dance.

So we do not lose hope. The prophetic is dangerous and comforting all at once, a warning of the wrath that is to come, and a promise of God's new day. The prophetic is a foretelling of future human/divine events.

The prophetic is good news for some and bad news for others. It engulfs the world as it is, and the world that lies ahead. Prophets say what they think, mean what they say, and the rest of us have to deal with it. They speak "truth to power," as we say these days, even when it literally costs them their heads.

Who is a prophet, who is not, and how do we you know the difference? That question echoes throughout both Testaments. Sometimes prophets are obvious—they seize the moment, address the times, and galvanize a culture. Sometimes their message is immediately clear and profound, at other times it is murky, and we wait on history for its verification, taking our chances in accepting it or ignoring it along the way. How do we verify the prophet and the message they proclaim?

In history, one person's prophet is another person's quack. Which of these folks would you accept as prophetically insightful: Thomas Helwys the Baptist? John Wesley the Methodist? Joseph Smith the Mormon? Mary Baker Eddy the Christian Scientist? Martin Luther King, Jr., the pastor/civil rights leader?

Even John the Baptist had his doubts about Jesus, of all people. Matthew says: "John, who was in prison, heard what Christ was doing, and sent his own disciples to put this question to him: 'Are you the one who is to come, or are we to expect someone else'" (Matt. 11:2–4). Someone else? Someone else? If John the Baptist were having second thoughts IN PRISON, then I don't feel so bad when Jesus stumps me as well.

But Jesus' response to John is a clue to the nature of the prophetic and its gospel ideal. He doesn't say: "Of course I am THE ONE, "God from God, Light from Light, true God from true God, Begotten not made, of one substance with the Father..." (that's the Nicene Creed three centuries later). Rather he says, "Tell John what you SEE and HEAR, the blind see, the lame walk, lepers are made clean, the deaf hear, the dead are raised to life, and the poor have received the good news." Then he adds, "Blessed are those who do not find me an obstacle to faith." Here are some signs of what the prophetic means, Jesus says. Now, John, you decide.

I guess John's not so scary once you really listen to Jesus. You see, there is a difference between these two prophets. John the Baptist says that "the Kingdom of God is on its way, prepare yourselves." Jesus says "the Kingdom is already here; live like you believe it." John Dominick Crossan writes that when Jesus says that the Kingdom is here, he means this: Heal those who are hurting and then eat with those who are healed.

And out of the healing and the eating will come a new community.[3] That's us! Let's dance.

---

[3] Crossan, *God & Empire,* 118. Crossan writes that Jesus is promoting "not just a vision or a theory but a praxis and a *communal* program, and that this program was not just for himself but for others as well.... Basically it was this: *heal the sick, eat with those you heal, and announce the Kingdom's presence in that mutuality.*"

# Finding Words, Finding Ourselves

## James 3:1–12; Mark 8:34–38

"They'll tell anything on you down in town." So says the old serpent-handling woman as she sits on her front porch in the Appalachian Mountains, killing flies and defending her church's beliefs from the sixteenth chapter of the Gospel of Mark. Serpent-handlers bear many burdens. From cheap novels, to academic treatises, to the Sally Jessie Rafael Show, serpent-handlers have been caricatured, analyzed, and criticized for their belief that the sacraments are alive and can kill you.

Whatever we might believe about handling snakes in church, we can agree with her about this: "They'll tell anything on you down in town," and sometimes in the Church of Jesus Christ. Face it, human beings, sanctified or unsanctified, can and do say terrible things about the way things are, about the way things ought to be, and about each other. We say too much or not enough. We don't always mean what we say, or we say what we really mean but to the wrong people. Sometimes we just say mean things. It is the tongue, so the book of James declares: "We use it to sing the praises of God, and we use it to invoke curses upon our fellow human beings who are made in God's likeness."

I confess that I often think we have little or nothing in common with the people of the idealized "New Testament Church," that mythic community we often seek to emulate but can't fully comprehend. The cultural differences are huge, aren't they? Electricity and automobiles, television and cell phones, computers and refrigerators, aspirin and antibiotics, not to mention Big Macs and Twitter, force us to keep our distance from their kind of world. If we tried to describe CDs, cellphones, airplanes, and Skype to them, they'd think such things incomprehensible, apocalyptic or demonic! They could be right! How dare we generalize from their times and culture to ours?

Today's biblical texts suggest otherwise. Cultural transitions abound, but our common humanity remains strangely intact. When James talks about "bridling the tongue" and when Jesus talks about losing your life and finding yourself, we know that some timeless questions haunt the human family.

To read the New Testament is to realize that "talking trash" affected the fledgling Christian communities as immediately and deeply as it does our own. Jesus ran into it soon enough. Remember his response to his early critics?

> How can I describe this generation? They are like the children sitting in the market place and shouting at each other, "We piped for you and you would not dance." "We wept and wailed, and you would not mourn." For John the Baptist came, neither eating nor drinking, and they say, "He is possessed." The son of Man came eating and drinking, and they say, "Look at him! A glutton and a drinker, a friend of tax-collectors, and sinners!" And yet God's wisdom is proved right by its results. (Matt. 11:19)

I've always loved that quick insight into first-century kid's culture and accompanying application. John was a teetotal grasshopper-eater who acted like a holiness prophet should act—harsh, direct, puritanical, and distant. Some followed his religion of repentance, but others thought he was difficult, if not crazy. Jesus, on the other hand, would drop by for happy hour—sip a nice little Manischewitz, but with the wrong kind of people—and the righteous crowd was scandalized.

Remember what the Corinthian Christians said when St. Paul showed up in town? "His letters have a literary flare, but when he appears he has no presence, and as a speaker he is beneath contempt" (2 Cor. 10:10–11). Amazing, isn't it? The first-century homiletic dilettantes let fly with words that stung Paul into this response: "I may be no speaker, but knowledge I have; at all times we have made known to you the full truth" (2 Cor. 11:5–6). (I once had a woman tell me that she hated my sermon so much she decided to give me the "evil eye" at the end of the service! When she showed up after that I tried to stay out of range.)

Disputes over words and actions were so serious in the early church that the Gospel of Matthew provides, from the mouth of Jesus, a formula for dealing with divisions and denunciations. "If someone sins against you," the text says, "take up the matter…strictly between yourselves." If that does not work, then "take one or two others with you, so that all facts may be duly established…." If that does not work, "report the matter to the congregation," "and if he will not listen even to the congregation," you must "treat him as you would a pagan or a tax-gatherer," (or a news analyst or a talk show host.) It appears that words were volatile enough, even with the first believers, that they needed a formula for mediating conflict. James was right. It takes a long time for our mouths to get "born again."

Did you notice? James doesn't give specific examples of the tongue's misuse. He understands that we all know what he was talking about. We've all "dished it out" and "taken it," maligned and been maligned with words. Perhaps we are worse off than our first-century counterparts because for us the tongue has been replaced with the computer keyboard. Early Christians could not "bridle" the tongue; we push "send" when we ought to push "delete." And once our words are sent, they can remain "online" forever. We are learning the hard way that emails, twitters, blogs and worst of all FACEBOOK are now the repositories of things we wish we'd not said in private let alone made public. One of the blights of the postmodern world is the cruelty being perpetrated, especially by young people, on the Internet. In fact, some suggest that online bullying and abuse may contribute to the suicide attempts of the iPhone, texting generation. Such viciousness does not travel just around the campus, it travels around the world.

We continually warn our students and ourselves: Don't put anything on the Internet that you don't want to haunt you all the days of your life. Lives and résumés built on years of community service or educational blood, sweat, and tears can be instantly damaged or destroyed when someone in Human Resources or on the search committee "Googles" you, and all your secrets are out. We may repent of what we say, but on the Web, we can never take it back.

We live, Bill Moyers says, in a "culture of cruelty" as far as cable stations and emails are concerned, unable to stop attacking one another, not simply because we disagree but because we make even the most benign disagreement a character issue. Talk shows, broadcast news, "reality TV" and the US Congress unbridle tongues for entertainment, evil and salaciousness hour by hour in our culture. We are a society overwhelmed by speeches in which "the truth" is nearly meaningless and mean words are nearly normative. While there is nothing new about verbal viciousness, we have the power to forward it globally in an instant—and never take it back.

We all struggle with words, inside and outside human relationships, words that bind up and break down, words that we hear ourselves saying and can't believe they are coming out of our mouths or our fingers. Our words can destroy as quickly as they bless—so we need strategies for governing our tongues and our text messages.

But let's not confuse cruel speech with issues of conscience. Our Baptist tradition reminds us that some things we can't keep silent about, even when it causes pain to ourselves, to others, and in our culture. Some things are so terrible, so hurtful, so unjust, and so broken that we cannot be silent. James is addressing cruelty, not conscience. He's not talking about "making nice" or selling out, or keeping silent about the horrors all around us. He is not silencing us in the face of injustice or indignation or the evils that must be addressed. Indeed, words we use to respond to such evil may get us in serious trouble with the church and the world. He's simply saying, don't waste your breath on hateful language—struggle with the truth and say what you must.

But avoiding moments of pettiness and cruelty in conversations often seems a losing battle, at least as James tells it. Biblical scholar Luke Johnson says: "James flatly asserts that no one can truly control speech (3:8)."[1]

I don't think there is much chance that many of us will do what James is demanding we do—bridle our tongues and the words they form. I just don't think it is in us, not all the time. Sooner or later our human DNA, even when it is "born again" compels us to say things we ought not to. So we have to face the music, endure the consequences, and hope to do better by grace. But beware, unbridled tongues and "open mikes" can and do end careers. These days the old adage "think before you speak" should include the warning: "and be sure the cell phone is turned off.

All this brings us to Jesus and his words in today's gospel text. In this passage, Jesus reminds his disciples that he knows exactly where his prophetic words will take him—to arrest, rejection, suffering, and crucifixion. "He spoke about it plainly," the gospel text says, colliding head on with James's admonition. They are words Peter cannot accept and he challenges their implications. And Jesus says it straight out: "Away with you, Satan, your thinking is not God's." Words have meaning: for our friends, our enemies, and ourselves. Jesus himself illustrates one of the great linguistic dilemmas of all our conversations:

---

[1] Luke Timothy Johnson, *The Book of James*, Anchor Bible 37A (New York: Doubleday, 1995) 264.

Are they simply harsh words required of volatile situations, or cruel words attacking persons with whom we disagree.

Then settling or extending the dilemma Jesus adds "to the people as well as his disciples": "Anyone who wishes to be a follower of mine must leave self behind, take up his cross, and come with me." Whoever cares for his own safety is lost; but whoever will be "lost for my sake and for the Gospel," is safe. "For what does a person gain by winning the whole world at the cost of the true self? What can …buy that self back?"

Whatever did he mean by that? Perhaps this: If the gospel is as radical as we say, it will re-form, transform, our entire self—identity, commitments, and words. Leaving self behind does not mean you stop being who you are, own up to who you are, warts, gifts, and all and find strategies for coming to terms with what you have found. It offers a strategy for relinquishing the glib nastiness, the cruel commentary, and the unsubstantiated rumor. It is to drop the power of self-destruction for the freedom of new insight into who we are and who we might become.

Frederick Buechner expands the words on today's bulletin when he writes: "Words are power, essentially the power of creation. By my words I both discover and create who I am. By my words I elicit a word from you."[2] I think the gospel message is this: You can't find yourself if you don't confront your words. We are free to say whatever we wish, I suppose, but doing so sometimes destroys/damages not only others, but something deep inside us. So if Jesus is right, then the transformation of our selves will help us to resist saying the hurtful, foolish, idiotic things that destroy, dehumanize, and overwhelm our relationships with others. And in finding our true selves perhaps we will strengthen our courage to resist, ignore, or endure the terrible words that people inevitably use on us. When you find yourself, you may find your voice and the courage to endure what they tell on you "down in town."

Several years ago, I heard the late Tom Hearn, then president of Wake Forest University, describe what he considered to be the three purposes for a university: to educate the young, to pursue research in a search for truth, and to nurture the civility of discourse. I have never forgotten that simple observation. Indeed, I try to remember it at every faculty meeting.

---

[2] Frederick Buechner, *Wishful Thinking* (New York: Harper & Row, 1979) 96.

So here's the deal: Taming the tongue is inseparable from finding the self. Maybe there is hope even for the most "unbridled" among us. The Psalmist, as usual, says it all: "Let the words of my mouth and the meditations of my heart, be acceptable in your sight, O God my strength and my redeemer." Tweet that, for God's sake. Amen.

# Having Second Thoughts?

## Psalm 84; John 6:56–69

"'I hear you are entering the ministry,' the woman said, looking down the long table, meaning no real harm. 'Was it your own idea, or were you poorly advised?'"[1] So Frederick Buechner describes his grandmother's first response when he told her that he was becoming a preacher. Apparently some of the "disciples" in today's Gospel text wondered if they had been similarly counseled. Maybe they started out with Jesus at the wedding in Cana of Galilee, in what John's Gospel calls the "first sign that he was the Messiah," when he took water and produced 180 gallons of top-flight cabernet. Or perhaps they were in "a large crowd" who followed him because of "the signs he performed in healing the sick." And surely some joined up when he said the blessing and fed the multitudes so thoroughly that twelve baskets of bread were left over (John 6:13).

But then he started all that talk about being the bread of life and declaring that, "whoever eats my flesh and drinks my blood possesses eternal life." And that's when "many of his disciples" decided they might have made a mistake. They said it straight up as the New English Bible translates it: "This is more than we can stomach! Why listen to such words?"

"More than we could stomach!" Jesus could generate a good controversy, couldn't he? Sometimes his actions get him in trouble—healing on the Sabbath, hanging out with "public sinners" and "winebibbers" (a great KJV word), or talking to women with questionable reputations—times when he stepped outside the boundaries of culture and religion. In today's text, however, his ideas create theological chaos and personal discomfort among those who loved him the most but often understood him the least. First he claims peculiar intimacy with God, and then gets into all that talk about eating flesh—his flesh—and drinking blood—his blood. This was a horrible concept for his listeners whose religion had

---

[1] Frederick Buechner, *The Alphabet of Grace* (New York: Seabury Press, 1970) 109.

serious guidelines about eating and drinking, "keeping kosher," we call it now, the proper preparation of animal flesh and blood. Here he comments on human flesh and blood, his own.

It is a complicated text. A vegan Moravian friend says that one communion Sunday when her son was around six years old, they read Jesus' words about "eating my flesh and drinking my blood" and when the elements were being passed her son whispered: "Mom, we can't eat this, we're vegetarians!"

Jesus' words when applied to Holy Communion divide us yet. Catholics and Lutherans take them literally, insisting that Christ is physically present in or alongside the bread and wine at communion. Other Protestants spiritualized or memorialized Jesus out of the bread and grape juice, asserting that his words in these texts are metaphors pure and simple. Pragmatic Swiss reformer Ulrich Zwingli insisted that when Jesus said of the bread, "This is my body," he didn't mean it literally. Jesus also said he was the door, Zwingli observed in a little sixteenth-century humor, but that didn't mean he really was one!

What seems clear is, as the KJV says poignantly: "From that time, many of his disciples went back, and walked no more with him" (John 6:66). Were they were having second thoughts? Did they wonder what they had gotten themselves into? When the good wine ran out, and the pithy little sayings got complicated, they had second thoughts.

What of us? Have we had second thoughts about Jesus, his Way and, of course, his church? Maybe not. Perhaps some among us set their hands to the gospel plow and never look back, experiencing Jesus and his call to new life and remaining clear and sure in that commitment all life long. But others of us struggle, I think, not just with what is said and done "in Jesus' name," but by Jesus himself. Lots of folks have second thoughts for lots of reasons. Let's not beat up on them too quickly. In fact, these days some people go looking for churches where second thoughts aren't just welcomed, but cultivated. So what gives us second thoughts anyway?

Some of us have second thoughts because Jesus, or following Jesus, is just so exhausting. Life is complicated enough without having to think about loving your enemy, turning the other cheek, going the extra mile, giving your possessions, even part of them, to somebody else. Then there is theology. In addition to loving your neighbor as yourself do we also have to comprehend the Trinity, Virgin Birth, Substitutionary-Ransom-

Moral-Influence theories of the atonement, the historical critical method of biblical studies and the premillennial dispensational theory of the atonement? We know those are grand ideas, that they bespeak high values, but it's just so much to negotiate, especially in a world where hunger, poverty, abuse, illness, cancer, and death are overpowering. It isn't that Jesus' teachings aren't meaningful; indeed they seemed so enticing and exciting when we first encountered them. But we get older and life gets more complex, and we are just too exhausted to keep doing the "Jesus thing" as a friend of mine calls it.

Others of us have second thoughts because there are so many choices and so many controversies involved in deciding how we want to follow Jesus and interpret his teaching, two thousand years later. It isn't that you can just follow Jesus, then and now, it is that you have to choose which Jesus you want to follow, "choose you this day" which Jesus you want to serve—Catholic Jesus, Baptist Jesus, Anglican Jesus, Pentecostal Jesus, Non-denominational Jesus. Republican Jesus, Democrat Jesus, Libertarian Jesus, or what about the Justice Jesus, the Marginalized Jesus, the celibate Jesus, the doctrinaire Jesus, the Prosperity Jesus, the don't-ask-don't-tell Jesus, or the women-can-do-everything-but-preach Jesus. Which Jesus is it, some of us ask, having second thoughts?

Still others of us think again because it seems that time and institutionalization has stolen the life out of "the old, old story, of Jesus and his love." His words, bursting out of the moment in first-century or second-century Galilee, got turned into "beliefs" about communion, election, predestination, or free will. We have second thoughts because the entitlement Jesus of much religious culture isn't radical enough. In a book called *The Meaning of Jesus,* historian Garry Wills says—I'm quoting from a review—"Christians don't understand Jesus' startlingly radical message so should not claim to have knowledge of how he would act today." (We can't know What Would Jesus Do?) So Wills says everyone "uses Jesus' words to rationalize a domesticated Christianity that upholds the status quo" or supports "discrimination towards those on the margins." Wills himself says some people have second thoughts about Christianity because it ignores the Jesus who "walks through social barriers and taboos as if they were cobwebs." Jesus is a radical mystery; but we tame him to make him manageable, and that causes some people to have second thoughts about the whole thing. Some people have walked away from Jesus because he is too dangerous; others, because he isn't dangerous enough.

It has happened across two centuries. Haven't you heard it (or thought it)—"I want to follow Jesus, I just can't stomach the Christians!" Christopher Hitchens nails us, frankly, in the book *God is Not Great*, running multiple lists of all the atrocities perpetuated in Jesus' name by his "disciples" for two thousand years. He writes that "until recently" when individuals challenged Christian belief or practice, "Christians could simply burn or silence anybody who asked any inconvenient questions."[2] Hitchens goes off on various inaccurate tangents, but not when he recounts the beheadings, burnings, imprisonments, and brutalities of Christian groups across the centuries. (Seems rather bleak this morning, doesn't it? We probably should have taken the offering earlier in the service today.)

And it goes on. My friend Joe Phelps, pastor of Highland Baptist church, Louisville, once hosted a community gathering called Honoring Sacred Texts, a response to all the craziness in the media over burning a Qur'an. His church was filled with Louisville folks, many of whom rose to read the texts that shape their lives in this moment in time. He received a couple of hundred emails denouncing his action. One read: "You are a pathetic excuse for a man.... You are truly a Judas and it would have been better for you to have never been born. I mean that in the most Christian way." With emails like that who wouldn't have second thoughts?

Don't despair quite yet. Suddenly the text takes a turn. Recognizing that disciples have indeed departed, Jesus asks the Twelve plaintively: "Will you also run away?" And Peter, as usual, is ready with a response that becomes a confession of faith: "To whom shall we go, Lord? YOU have the words of eternal life!" I don't know how you read that text, but to me there is an element of desperation about it. "If not you, who?" Peter pleads. While some thought better of it and walked away, Peter cannot let it go. He has staked everything on Jesus, or is at least beginning to do so.

"Jesus," he says, "we've got no where else to go." Maybe they were all just tired; tired of the crowds, tired of the complexity, so bone tired

---

[2] Christopher Hitchens, *God Is Not Great* (New York: Twelve, 2007) 115.

that Peter could not bear to think that he had to go through another quest with another would-be messiah.

And that is the twist in today's text. Sometimes the second thoughts come from the people on the other side of the argument that can't bear another day of living outside the gospel. Their lives are so full of deep hurts and bad choices, terrible betrayals and lost hope that they have nowhere else to go. If this doesn't work, then it is all over anyway, and suddenly, unexpectedly Jesus makes sense. Some people have second thoughts about their lives and walk into, not away from, the gospel. It happens, you know.

At least once a year I try to reread *The Long Loneliness*, the autobiography of Dorothy Day, founder of the Catholic Worker Movement. The title of her book describes what she calls the "first part of my life," secular journalist, passionate Socialist, living in the Bohemian environs of Greenwich Village of the 1920s, able to drink Eugene O'Neill under the table, so they said. She wrote: "During that time I felt the spell of the long loneliness descend on me. In all that great city of seven millions, I found no friends; I had no work; I was separated from my fellows. Silence in the midst of city noises oppressed me. My own silence, the feeling that I had no one to talk to overwhelmed me so that my very throat was constricted; my heart was heavy with unuttered thoughts; I wanted to weep my loneliness away."[3] The long loneliness, and pregnancy in a common-law marriage led to second thoughts about her life and turned her to Christ and his church, confessing: "My very existence as a radical, my whole make-up, led me to want to associate myself with others, with the masses, in loving and praising God."[4]

Sometimes second thoughts go the other way, from folks who cannot stomach one more day of the long loneliness or the self-destructive habits, and faith takes root. Sooner or later some people, no, let's just say all of us, get so beat up, so broken, so overwhelmed we need to be "saved" (can I use that much abused, misused word?) from all

---

[3] Dorothy Day, *The Long Loneliness: An Autobiography* (San Francisco: Harper & Row, 1952) 51.

[4] Ibid., 139.

that is destroying us. It is easy to have our own second thoughts about Jesus. He is exhausting, isn't he? Exasperating, too. Thank God.

# His Word Has Found a Home

## John 5:31–47

Okay, let's agree that this is a difficult passage of scripture assigned for our Lenten series today. Jesus speaks harshly. The Word that became flesh and is full of "grace and truth" talks pretty sharply about his own people. He lays out his credentials, not testifying "on my own behalf," but letting others—John the Baptizer specifically—do it for him. But, says Jesus, "I rely on a testimony higher than John's" and moves immediately to his direct "accreditation" by God—the "Father who sent me," he says. And then he "stops preaching and goes to meddling" as the old preachers used to say. He directs his strong words, his condemnation, really, to his own people, the folks who reared him, taught him, heard him, criticized him, and obsessed over him. Jesus confronts them in this passage with some fascinating statements. The one that haunts me today—never having ventured into this text until now—is this: "And the Father who has sent me has borne witness on my behalf. His voice you have never heard, his form you have never seen; *his word has found no home in you* because you do not believe in the one whom he sent."

"His word has found no home in you." That is a phrase worth spending some time with on our way to Golgotha, on the way to Calvary, on the way to Easter.

Here is where we start. If we want to make this only about "the Jews," if we want to perpetuate that kind of division, then we should all go home feeling pretty good about ourselves—the new people of God, the ones grafted onto Abraham's seed (as St. Paul says), the ones who recognized something that Jesus' contemporaries did not. If Jesus' denunciation is all about "them" and has little or nothing to do about "us," then let's have a prayer, feel good about ourselves (some might call that self righteousness or pride) and go eat lunch half way to the empty tomb.

But what if this phrase "his word has found no home in you" is not about "them" but about all of us—all of us who brush up against Jesus like "they" did by the Sea of Galilee or on the Mount of Olives—and look beyond him. We are the ones who look but do not see; hear but do know understand; believe but do not live by faith. If you want this passage to mean something, then take it to heart, here and now.

Today in this Lenten service, let's ask the reverse of Jesus' harsh words: When is it that God's word has found a home in us? That is the Lenten question. This text and the journey to Calvary point me to these two affirmations:

God's word has found a home in us when we:

1. Accept our need of grace
2. Decide to walk—better yet struggle with—the Jesus Way.

To read this text is to realize that sometimes grace shows up all around us and we do not have "eyes to see and ears to hear." Sometimes we become so self-sufficient, so sure of our own insights and abilities, and we forget that so much of life is gift—things we didn't create or things we didn't even deserve. We think we are "self-made" men and women who owe no one, need no one, rely on no one. Some folks think it is "all about them," that the world revolves around their little universe as if they deserve everything and need no one. They are the users of the world who take from others and give little in return. There is no room for grace in their existence—it is only entitlement.

That can happen in religious communities. In fact, one of the great dangers of religion is that it can keep us from grace. In today's text Jesus is speaking about the religious crowd that can show up in anybody's synagogue, church house, or mosque. For these folks religious rules, religious dogma, religious rituals, religious identity (all appropriate in proper perspective) can become fences that wall them off from grace. The worst kind of religion is the kind that blinds us to the unexpected presence of God in ourselves and in the world.

Remember that Jesus was a practitioner of the religion of his day. He went "habitually" to the synagogue, the Bible says, and "up to the Temple," when in Jerusalem. But he challenged those rules of his religion that closed the door to grace—healing on the Sabbath because hurt needed to be dealt with no matter how holy the day might be; challenging all forms of religion that dehumanized and ignored "the least of these." Grace is all around us, and we need to look beyond corpse-cold religion to see it.

But sometimes grace is stalled, not by us, but by our experience of the world. Sometimes life comes at us with a vengeance and we are blinded to grace, not because we resist it, but because things are so bad that they blur our vision.

Recently, I preached at a church where the consistent confession used throughout the morning service is this (I'm sure you've heard it before): "God is good." And the congregation answers back: "All the time." Well, I appreciate that confession and think it is appropriate. For myself, however, I wish that every time we offer it, we would add one more phrase: "God is good. All the time." And then I wish we'd add: "Life is hard. All the time." I think that would take the edge off the possibility of making a too-easy confession of God's goodness.

You see, life pushes all of us, sooner or later, in ways that may distance us from grace. And that is when we need the community of faith. Sometimes the strength and grace of others carries us to grace when our own eyes and lives are too blurred to see it. Truth is, is we are ever gifted—graced—by people and events that shape us and carry us, even when we or they do not know it. God's Word has found a home in us when we recognize and cling to our need of grace.

One final observation: God's word has also found a home in us when we decide to follow—better yet struggle with—the Jesus Way. I think that idea is at the heart of today's text. The people around Jesus, his own people, his family, his heritage was divided over who he was and what he meant, and in the Gospel of John, Jesus has some harsh things to say to them. But there were some people, then and now, who decided to take a chance on Jesus, take a chance on grace. Last summer, as most of you know, our father, the reverend Darryl Aaron and I joined Reverends Prince Rivers, James Cook, Chris Chapman, and Amy Dean, among other ministers in this region, and spent two weeks in Israel. One of those weeks we walked every day "by the Sea of Galilee," and I found myself haunted by the memory of those who, as the Bible says, "left their nets" and followed Jesus. Their gamble, their risk was no easier or harder than our own, just different. They saw him in the flesh, heard his words audibly, and touched him in the breaking of bread by the seashore. But he was the same person that others thought was a huge fraud, a rebel rabbi, a false messiah. We aren't in his physical presence, but we have the post-Easter, two-thousand-year testimony of Jesus and the church. But for them and for us it was ever a risk.

"He came unto his own," John's gospel says earlier, "and his own received him not." Some people still can't believe the story is true, or the grace sufficient, or the hope sure and certain. "But," John adds, "to as many as did receive him, to those he gave the privilege of becoming sons and daughters of God" (John 1:11-12).

So today, on the way to Easter, in the delivery room, in the emergency room, and in the hospice room, let us look for and welcome God's good grace. Let us open our lives so that the "Word can find a home in us." Let us receive that word, and cling to it, until we all go home.

# Lamenting and Adapting Then and Now

## Psalm 79:1–8; Jeremiah 8:18–9:1; Luke 16:1–9

I love the lectionary, that collection of biblical texts used throughout the Christian year to carry the church across the scriptures on a three-year cycle. I hate the lectionary, that collection of biblical texts that compels the church to confront biblical texts we'd just as soon ignore. In fact, growing up Baptist, I never had to visit those uncomfortable texts until I got to a Methodist College (Texas Wesleyan). Some Baptist churches use the lectionary these days, thank God, but many do not. We do "drive-by" preaching—running through the Bible, grabbing those texts that come most easily. Methodists go inside and order off the menu! We Baptists, therefore, don't have to confront the Bible until the Methodists and the Lectionary force us to do so—like today.

The lectionary today offers some of the most uncivil texts available, all mixed together. From the Psalms to Jeremiah to Luke's gospel, we are greeted with unbearable times, unquenchable grief, and unabashed manipulation, all in the name of God. The texts are uncivil; they probably shouldn't be in the Bible, not if we want to make everything fit, promise escape from every evil, and deliverance from every pain and terror. But here they are, reminding us of what theologian David Tracy taught us years ago: The genius of ancient texts is that they resist domestication; they carry us where we do not wish to go; they remind us of things we'd just as soon forget; they lament the way things really are.

So without further ado let's see where these texts might take us. Since I'm a stranger here it probably can't hurt, but I've parked my car near the door nonetheless. Here's the thesis of this morning's sermon, drawn from three of the most uncivil texts available. Life is difficult; disaster can occur at any moment in events beyond our control and of our own creation; so learn to live in those realities. Indeed, today's biblical texts offer a clear, if troubling, strategy for dealing with life's terrible moments: lament and adapt. These ancient writers did it then (when life's difficulties descended) and we can learn to do it now in times different but no less certain than the people who wrote these terrible words so long ago.

Listen to the Psalmist's lament, sung out in synagogues and churches for three thousand years, a sober hymn if ever there was one. "The heathen have invaded your domain, God.... The dead bodies of your servants they have thrown out as food for the birds; ...Around Jerusalem their blood is spilt like water and there is no one to give them burial" (Ps. 79:1–4). If I lived in Baghdad, I might read that Psalm every morning to give voice to the realities all around—Darfur, too, perhaps, or Kabul. But I could have sung it on the campus of Virginia Tech University after the shootings, or in New Orleans after Katrina, or last week, even. I could sing it in Davie County, North Carolina on almost any Sunday morning after some local teens wrapped their car/s around assorted trees on any given Saturday night.

Life is ever so fragile. It can take a turn at any minute on the Interstate, in the emergency room, in the living room, with a suicide bombing, after the tornado, or in the local bar. Every day we open the newspaper to catastrophes large and small that have descended on our neighbors or our world and we hope and pray we can dodge another bullet in our own families and personal lives. But they find us all, sooner or later and with the Psalmist we lament the terrible times of our existence.

The Bible is full of people lamenting the times of their lives, crying out to God for relief, but unbearably honest about what is going on around them. Laments are often not very "Christian"—they do not try to make everything fit, everything nice and spiritual. Like this Psalm, the lamentations of many biblical writers tell it like it is, acknowledge that bad things happen to good and bad people. They often call down fire and brimstone on their enemies. In today's lesson, the Psalmist beseeches God: "Pour out your wrath on nations that do not acknowledge you." Not a very pluralistic response to the moment. Sometimes the lamentations even cast doubts on the trustworthiness of God, no matter how powerful or loving the deity may claim to be. "How long, Lord, will you be roused to such fury?" These people do not "make nice" with their enemies or with God. It is a terrible time, and the rage of the oppressed boils over. Sometimes things are so overwhelming and we are so in need of deliverance that woe be to those who get in our way, even God. This is religion that is neither pretty nor easy. It is raw and raging, looking for God and tormented by enemies.

And then there is Jeremiah—a prophet living amid terrible invasion of an unwelcome people—the Babylonians—who cart off captives, desecrate holy places, and destroy hope. Jeremiah tells God exactly what he is feeling: "There is no cure for my grief." Indeed, he asks, "is there no balm, no ointment, no aloe, no antibiotic in the land that will cure us?"

Are these ancient peoples the only ones who know this kind of pain? Hardly. These verses, then and now, remind us of the layers of stress that fall on us, or can fall on us at any moment, any day. Some stress is temporary. It hits us hard in illness or accident, but we get through it—not without difficulty—but we get through it. The chemo works; the surgery is a success; the therapy and the marriage hold; we can see our way through to the other side. (The church, by the way, is very good at dealing with temporary stress, the things we can get people through.)

But other stress is chronic. It will not go away; it changes our lives forever, and forces us to come to terms with new realities even as we lament the situation. We work hard for ourselves or on behalf of others; we do everything we can possibly do; we go through every treatment, every rehab, every counselor, but the disability is permanent, the cure doesn't work, and the marriage can't be put back together, and we hear ourselves shouting inside, often in the wee hours of the mornings, Jeremiah's ancient question of himself and God: "Why has no new skin grown over the wound?" Can you be more dramatic, more specific, than that? THEN we learn about lamentations. And, at least at times, it is lamentation that gets us through the night.

In the summer after 9/11, I attended a conference in which religious leaders from New York City discussed the impact of those terrible events on their respective religious communions. One, an evangelical Christian, said that one of the first thing his worshiping communion had to do was drop the praise choruses with their shouts of expectation, healing, and joy, and replace them with some of the older, more somber hymns that took seriously the depths and sorrows of life. Their praise choruses had a ring of superficiality at a time when they needed to acknowledge the depths of pain and loss. "Could my tears forever flow / Could my zeal no languor know?"[1] OR perhaps we sing: "'Tis midnight and on Olive's brow / the star is dimmed that lately shone, / 'Tis midnight in the garden now, / the suff'ring Savior prays alone."[2]

The other religious leader spoke of his more liberal congregation that had exorcized many / most of the hymns that seemed too depressing or too prone to emphasize human evil and godlessness. They were forced back to those hymns that gave voice to the reality of intentional sin in the world: "I love the cross of Jesus, it tells me what I am, / A vile and guilty creature, saved only through the Lamb. / No righteousness nor merit no beauty can I plead; / Yet in the cross I glory, my title there I read."[3] Or Charles Wesley's words: "Now incline me to repent; / let me now my fall lament; / deeply my revolt deplore, / weep, believe and sin no more."[4] Some of life's terrible, unpredictable moments compel us to revisit the limits of our own theologies—the areas we've left undone.

Churches should give serious attention to ministry to those individuals and families who live every day of their lives amid chronic stress—life situations that will not go away and that cannot be gotten through. Sometimes all they can do is hold on, and the faith of the believing, worshiping, consciously caring community helps them hold on. In the church I attend here in Winston-Salem, the deacons lead the central, pastoral prayer of each Sunday service. One old deacon starts his prayers in a most basic way: "Lord, we thank you that you woke us up this morning, and that we are clothed and in our right minds." I love that prayer—because it reminds me that sometimes all you can cling to are the basics and hope for the best. Sometimes we rejoice to be awake and fully clothed! (I sometimes remind the deacon that I could never tell God that in a room full of Baptists, they were all in their right minds! It is a statistical impossibility.)

Which brings us to Jesus and this ridiculous parable sometimes identified as the story of "the unjust steward," better called the parable of the manipulative, conniving, despicable, creep. Jesus could tell a story, couldn't he? And this one is no exception. Years ago I left a theological

---

[1] Augustus M. Toplady, "Rock of Ages, Cleft for Me," *The Baptist Hymnal* (Nashville: Convention Press, 1991) 342.

[2] William B. Tappan, "'Tis Midnight and on Olive's Brow," *Baptist Hymnal*, (Nashville: Convention Press, 1956) 106.

[3] Frederick Whitefield, "I Saw the Cross of Jesus," *The Baptist Hymnal*, 286.

[4] Charles Wesley, "Depth of Mercy," *The Baptist Hymnal*, 306).

seminary, where I had taught for sixteen years, for a university where I was to teach undergraduates. The faculty sent word that after teaching church history to graduate students for years I needed to teach New Testament to freshmen and sophomores. I agreed, with fear and trembling, and called a friend who has taught undergrads for years, telling him that I knew little of the New Testament for purpose of teaching it in any systematic way. "You can do it," he said. "I'll send you my notes." Then he joked: "By the way, you don't have to know nothing to teach freshmen and sophomores." Turned out he was mostly right.

So I reread the New Testament to teach it, and here's what I discovered that I had never seen before in the Gospels:

First, in so many of Jesus' stories, the people who think they know everything about God know very little, and the people who you think would never be saved, wind up being the line leaders. (You know, Good Samaritans, bad tax collectors, and libidinous prodigal sons.) Second, how many strong, indeed, aggressive women there are in Jesus' life, such as Mary: "Lord, if you had been here my brother would not have died"; the Canaanite women: "But Lord, even the dogs eat the crumbs from the master's table"; and his own mother: "Child," she says to the son of God, "Why have you treated us like this? Your father and I have looked everywhere for you." Third, how many of Jesus' stories have to do with economics, economics, economics—lost coins, lost sheep, spendthrift sons, and unjust stewards?

Today's parable gives us two of the three of those gospel tendencies—a bad character becomes the hero, and it is all about the money. The story is simple: A CEO hears complaints that his money manager is mishandling funds, so he asks for an accounting then fires him. The manager is nothing if not manipulative and self-serving—did you hear that great line: "too weak to dig, too proud to beg." (If you sometimes fit that description, signify by the uplifted hand.) So he does what he does best: he adapts to his new situation, cuts deals with the constituents and, Jesus says he was so "astute" that the master wound up admiring him. The text concludes: "For in dealing with their own kind the children of this world are more astute than the children of light." That gospel truism is as valid now as it was then.

What a disgusting story for Jesus to tell, what a lesson—Here is my take on this complicated text I'd just as soon ignore—there are times when life strikes so hard that there is no going back. Even amid the lamentations, we are forced to learn to adapt. How many young people are returning from Iraq lamenting and adapting to war injuries, artificial limbs, limited access, lost faculties? How many people lamenting divorce or death of a spouse learn, ever so slowly and painfully, to adapt to the realities of a new situation, even when the stress is temporary or chronic?

Three decades ago in April, a doctor in Massachusetts walked into my spouse's hospital room shortly after she had given birth to our beautiful blond daughter and said, "Sorry, but we've got to keep her for observations for awhile. There are some problems." Thirty-plus years later, our dear daughter Stephanie works in a wonderful respite care program at Centenary United Methodist Church that fits her special needs nicely. We've spent all this time adapting to Stephanie's needs as we both lament and celebrate her struggles and her gifts. We learned to live differently than we ever expected to live.

Jesus' awful parable of the creepy steward perhaps says this: Life can take a turn, sometimes because of nothing we have done, or sometimes because of difficulties of our own creation. When it does, we don't have to like it. We can shout, cuss (did I say cuss?), get in God's face and God will not be threatened for a moment (or at least shouldn't be).

When life goes sour (as it will sooner or later), are we as "astute" as this worthless character in rising amid the rubble of pain and hopelessness? Well, we are "children of light," aren't we? Well, aren't we?

# Loaves, Fishes, and Krispy Kremes: Unanticipated Wonder

## Matthew 14:13–21

This homily, or whatever it is, began on a recent morning after I had just polished off two Krispy Kreme donuts, purchased straight from the assembly line, hot and fresh. I ate both of them in the car before I got out of the parking lot. And they were wonderful. For a long time I hated Krispy Kremes, but that was because I ate them cold, out of a box purchased at some convenience store or from the ROTC or frat guys selling them on campus as a fund-raising project. Never, I mean never (if you can possibly help it), eat Krispy Kremes cold. They should only be eaten direct from the little rollers in the official Krispy Kreme shop with the big neon sign on the window flashing HOT DONUTS evangelically throughout the day. There is one of those little Kingdom of God stores less than a mile from my house. Indeed, I live in Winston-Salem, North Carolina, the home of Krispy Kreme, the donut that continues to take America by storm. When Krispy Kreme hit Manhattan, it soon rivaled the bagel (heaven forbid) as the nosh-of-choice in the Big Apple. My mother even sent me clippings from the Fort Worth (Texas) *Star-Telegram* detailing the fact that Krispy Kreme glazed are now challenging biscuits and breakfast burritos in that city "where the West begins." If Fort Worth has fallen, can Abilene be far behind?

Why all the uproar? Because, believe it or not, hot (I am a purist here) Krispy Kremes are the almost perfect blend of all the wrong substances—sugar, flour, glaze, and FAT—in a most absolutely irresistible delicacy. They are, I believe, one of life's unanticipated wonders—those little moments when the sweetness is palpable and real. But one leads to two, and two to three, and then it's over. The only way to protect yourself is to buy only two and run out of the store as quickly as possible. If you ask for three or more, the sales person may say—and they really do say this—"Don't you know they are cheaper by the dozen?" And since every American loves a bargain, we go for a dozen.

A friend recalls his student days at Wake Forest University, when he and his roommate would go to Krispy Kreme at 2 a.m. on Wednesday mornings and hit the buy-a-dozen-get-a-dozen-free special. Then they would each eat 12 HOT donuts before they got back to the dorm, which means they ate one Krispy Kreme, approximately every 0.2 miles. (They graduated and are now in their early 50s, so it must not be terminal, yet.) On a recent business trip to New York City, two of my Wake Forest colleagues (including a Moravian woman who should have known better) hit the Manhattan streets at 2 a.m. on a Krispy Kreme Kuest. They found the place and ate to their hearts' content—unanticipated wonder on the dark streets of Manhattan.

Wonder, the dictionary says, is "That which arouses awe, astonishment, surprise, or admiration; a marvel."[1] Wonder, I think, is at the heart of thankfulness. It is gratitude for those moments in life that we treasure, even, especially, when we do not fully understand them. Wonder is one important response to grace gifts we do not deserve, but receive with joy.

Was it wonder that the Israelites experienced on the mornings in the wilderness with the manna? Did the "manna" consumed by the wayward Hebrews after their deliverance from Egypt have properties of Krispy Kreme about it? Hear the reading of the word of God, and consider the biblical texts for yourselves: "When dew fell on the camp at night the manna would fall with it" (Num. 11:9). And, "The people went about collecting it to grind in handmills to pound in mortars; they cooked it in a pot and made it into cakes, which tasted like butter-cakes," BUTTER-CAKES?? (Num. 11:8). And, said Moses: "Each of you is to gather as much as he can eat.... The Israelites did this, ...Each had just as much as he could eat." (Exod. 16:16–17) And, "Moses said, No one is to keep any of it till morning. Some, however, did not listen to him; they kept part of it till morning, and it became full of maggots and stank, and Moses was angry with them." (Exod. 16:19–20) And, "Each morning every one gathered as much as was needed; it melted away when the sun grew hot." (Exod. 16:21)

I rest my case. Anyone who knows anything about Krispy Kremes and their brief but delicious existence must acknowledge the resemblance. Krispy Kreme as manna...is there a "sermon" in that? Probably not, but I wonder.... Sometimes, as much as I hate to admit it, I need a little Krispy Kreme religion, moments when there is a surge of

---

[1] William Morris, *The American Heritage Dictionary* (Boston: Houghton Mifflin Co., 1978), 1472.

warmth and vitality, when the "deliciousness" of grace catches me off guard, sweeps away my defense mechanisms, and simply lets me celebrate the goodness of God—moments when I experience "a marvel." I need occasions when the (forgive me here) sugar-high of the Spirit makes me feel braver, and maybe better than I really am—at least for a moment.

All the great religious traditions have such moments: At the Jewish feast of Purim, my Birmingham friend, Rabbi Jonathan Miller, often dresses up like cookie monster, celebrating to high heaven the moment Esther saved the people of God; at Pentecost we Christians delight in the coming of the Holy Spirit. My first visit to the renovated Cathedral of the Assumption after moving from Louisville came on a Pentecost Sunday when the baptismal fount bubbled with baptisms and multiple generations crowded into that sacred space, and I couldn't control the tears. Several years ago, a group of whirling dervish Muslims took Wake Forest University by storm, and their dances unleashed joy in all who saw and heard them. We thank God for those moments when our communities let their collective hair down in gladness.

But I can't live on Krispy Kremes forever. Indeed, like the children of Israel with manna, if that's all you eat, after awhile, even Krispy Kremes will get boring. See where I'm headed with all this? Krispy Kreme religion is great and absolutely necessary from time to time. But it won't sustain for the long haul. It won't compensate or substitute for the hard sayings all our traditions bear about doing unto others, going the extra mile, turning the other cheek, visiting the prisoners, and bringing "good news to the poor." Grace, like donuts, may be "cheaper by the dozen" but it's no good at all if you have to bargain for it.

This brings us to this brief gospel text. Matthew says that Jesus is overtaken in some "lonely place" by the crowds who desperately need him. "And he cured them," scripture says. And when they got hungry, he fed them, not with treats, but with the common food at hand, five loaves and two fishes. And I love the New English Bible here: "And they all ate to their hearts content." And unanticipated wonder surrounded them, not in sugar and spice, but in salty fish and pita bread. And when they were done, they collected the pieces and, I guess, had some more for later. In common hunger and stick-to-the-ribs food they found room for gratitude and wonder.

Perhaps we need to celebrate the wonder of the mundane, the wonder of another day, of daily bread, of life that is special because it is also ordinary. Grace, at its essence, is unanticipated, evident in the explosive surprises, and in the oh-so-common. Perhaps personally and collectively, spiritually and theologically, we need both metaphors don't we? We need the wonder of the sugar-high celebrations, and the strength to live with the mundane, daily-ness of it all. I've taken communion like that, haven't you? There have been occasions—at Canterbury Cathedral and up a hollow in an Appalachian meeting house, when the place and the moment brought wonder and a sense of the absolute joy of faith. But there have been other times when the Spirit showed up where least expected.

When we lived in Boston, I was minister at a small community church where, in my first month, a deacon and I took communion to long-time members Joe and Bessie Blake. They'd been married for more than sixty years and when I met them, Bessie was dealing with a chronic heart condition. As it turned out, this would be her last communion in this world. The deacon couldn't find the communion kit so he whipped out a bottle of Welch's Grape Juice, poured it into paper cups, and handed each of us cracker. But we spoke of body and blood, of life and death, and when it was over, Bessie said, "Joe, let's sing the doxology." Years later even to tell the story is to return to the unanticipated wonder of that audacious moment, with two people long dead now, but not forgotten. To sing and pray and hold on to each other in the midst of the mundane is to acknowledge that God is present even when we don't feel anything, when faith is dormant, but present, nonetheless.

What does this mean? (Perhaps nothing—Krispy Kremes may not be a good metaphor.) But perhaps it means that we all need to cut the Spirit some slack, never knowing how it may find us. Good religion can be present when you can feel it, and when you can't. The trick is to be open to the unanticipated wonder of grace.

So let's unleash some joy tonight, because for a moment at least some Protestants, Catholics, Jews, Muslims, Hindus, Buddhists, and others decided to sing and pray together. And in a world where that is not all that common, and in a country where churches, mosques, and synagogues are still burned and even shot at, let us commit ourselves to the long haul in the name of peace, and learning, and love. If some of us get a little high from it, that's great. But if some of us don't, that's ok, too.

So go in peace, and as you are going know this: Unlike Krispy Kremes, faith will keep till morning. Good News. Amen.

# Worldliness and Wonder[1]

## Luke 2:1–20

And it came to pass in those days that there went out a decree from Caesar Augustus that all the world should be taxed. And that taxing was first made when Cyrenius was governor of Syria. And all went to be taxed, everyone unto his own city. And Joseph also went up from Galilee out of the city of Nazareth, unto Judea into the city of David which is called Bethlehem, because he was of the house and lineage of David, to be taxed with Mary his espoused wife, being great with child. And so it was that while they were there the days were accomplished that she should be delivered. And she brought forth her firstborn son and wrapped him in swaddling cloths and laid him in a manger because there was no room for them in the inn. And there were in the same country, shepherds abiding in the fields keeping watch over their flocks by night, and lo the angel of the Lord came upon them and the glory shown round about them and they were sore afraid.

I could say more (from memory), but I'd just be showing off. That ancient story, taken from Luke's Gospel in the King James Version of the Bible, entered my memory long before I learned to read the story itself. It haunts me yet, a classic Christian drama full of worldliness and wonder all at once. The worldliness was there from the beginning. The very grace of God "becomes flesh" not in some idyllic Eden or ethereal Oz but in the harsh realities of a world at once so far away and so very near to our own. Yet it is so filled with wonder that even Jesus' mother can't take it all in, all at once: "Mary kept all these things," Luke wrote, "and pondered them in her heart." Tonight, together, maybe we should too.

Ponder this: Jesus was born in Bethlehem because of taxes. His family actually lived in _____ (this is an interactive sermon) but we sing "O Little town of Bethlehem" because of "a decree from Caesar Augustus that all the world should be taxed." The events we recall

---

tonight with coffee, bread, and candles began in a world dominated by imperial armies, government policy, and economics, economics, economics. What's changed? As the New Testament tells it, God shows up in the flesh while his family is looking for the Bethlehem branch of H&R Block! Jesus' birth is inseparable from first-century Roman tax policy. Can his story get more "worldly" than that?

Actually, it can. Ponder this late Elizabethan rendering of a scandalous text: "espoused wife, being great with child." If I were writing a Gospel, I don't believe I would have mentioned that! Yet the text says straight out that by first-century standards the woman we call the Blessed Virgin Mary was a not-yet-married, but very pregnant, probably teenage transient giving birth to the savior of the world in the parking lot of a Bethlehem Motel VI! (That's a Roman numeral.) Suddenly the story isn't just worldly, it is downright earthy!

She was one tough woman, that Mary of Nazareth, singing radical, politically incorrect songs with the first pangs of morning sickness. In Luke chapter one when the angel tells her what lies ahead, Mary chants what we call the Magnificat, a hymn full of worldliness and wonder, half praise chorus, half socio-economic manifesto. The New English Bible sings it like this:

> Tell out, my soul, the greatness of the Lord; rejoice, rejoice my spirit in God my savior. For God has regarded the low estate of his hand maiden, lowly as she is. From henceforth all generations will call me blessed, so great is God's mercy, the Lord the Holy one.
>
> God's name is holy, with mercy sure from generation to generation. The deeds of God's strong right hand have gotten the victory.
>
> The arrogant of heart and mind God has scattered. He has torn imperial powers from their thrones, but the humble have been lifted up. God has filled the hungry with good things; the rich sent away empty. (Luke 1:46–53)

The way his Mama tells it, Jesus' birth has implications for those who have nothing and those who have everything. It is not simply about salvation in some other kingdom by and by, but how we live in the real world here and now. If we want to "keep Christ in Christmas" let's stop being arrogant, learn some humility, and do all we can to fill the hungry with good things. And since right now one out of four children in the United States of America is on food stamps, we'd better hurry.

Make no mistake about it the Blessed Virgin Mary was tough as nails. I don't think for a moment that she rode a donkey the thirty miles from Nazareth to Bethlehem. I think she walked the whole way great with child, the baby Jesus kicking in her belly with every step.

Now ponder this: "There were in the same country shepherds among the fields." Isn't it just like God to announce good news to the world not at a cocktail party hosted by Caesar Augustus, but in the fields with the Bedouins, a bunch of nomads on the margins of society? Let's ask ourselves tonight: who are the people in the same country with us, on the margins of our geography who have heard God's good news in ways we never noticed?

Was Mary right after all? "God has torn imperial powers from their thrones but the humble have been lifted up." Luke's Gospel calls attention to the God who colors outside the box—who can't be controlled, and who shows up with the folks no one expected. It suggests that grace is not an entitlement; it is an unanticipated gift, often revealed through the unseen, overlooked people who occupy the same country as the rest of us.

And by the way, the shepherds were sore afraid: In fact, the angels seemed to have scared the heaven out of them. We've made the story of the baby so comfortable, and so manageable, haven't we? We've tamed it considerably with two millennia of retelling that it doesn't scare us at all. We've piped the angels' songs into the mall, fretting less that God has come to us, than that some bone-tired clerk will forget to wish us Merry Christmas after taking our Visa Cards at the temple of mammon. But the radical word to the humble and the hungry brought by the Bethlehem baby hardly startles us at all. He grew up, you know, Jesus of Nazareth, and his talk about turning the other cheek, going the extra mile, loving your enemies and your neighbor as your self ought to scare us toward transformation in a world where people still treat each other like trash and often do it in the name of somebody's god. Perhaps the advent season should make us all sore afraid, at least momentarily, because of all the things we "have done that we ought not to have done, and the things we have left undone in this worldly mess we call humanity, a race wondrously created in the image of God.

And to top it all off, the Christ child enters the world with an impossible agenda: and on earth peace. And in those words wonder and worldliness collide. Two thousand years later there is still no real peace

111

in Bethlehem, let alone on the entire earth! The military checkpoints in Bethlehem remain; it is only the soldiers who have changed. Tonight we'll nibble some spicy buns, sip some super-sweet coffee, light some beeswax candles, and even try to praise God in the highest, but Peace on Earth, are you kidding?

And that's the wonder of it. Tonight, we are compelled to sing that long and lonely peace song because we've got no choice, in a world filled with weapons even the ruthless Roman legions could never even have imagined. So we cling to the words of the grown up Jesus: "How blessed are the peacemakers, for they shall be called children of God."

The wonder of the Bethlehem story is that in Christ hope is possible, not as wishful thinking but in the determination that, against all odds, we can work for transformation on this earth. It is the same hope Mary felt when her water broke a long way from home. It is the hope of shepherds who came with haste to find "this thing that the Lord has made known unto us." It is the hope of a wondrous and worldly peace that includes not only the dominant species but also whales and leopards, spotted owls and drowning polar bears. It is the hope that through hard work and good grace, women and men of goodwill really can decide, "to study war no more." For if the wonder of that ancient anthem, glory to God in the highest and on earth peace, continues to elude us, then we had better be sore afraid, don't you think? Ponder that with the coffee, the buns, and the beeswax, for God's sake. Amen.

# Jacob: Wrestling with Strangers

## (And anybody else who comes along)

I attended my first snake handling in June 1990. (Just wanted to be sure I had your attention.) It was a celebrative affair—a kind of family reunion, dinner on the ground, revival meeting, and serpent-handling all rolled into one. The event was held on a sultry Sunday morning up a holler, so Appalachians say, not far from Berea College where I was teaching that summer. The service was outdoors—thank God. One's first experience of the serpent-handlers should best be outdoors (think about it). It began with a communal prayer and everybody kneeling on the hard ground, many praying out loud, simultaneously. The singing—accompanied by guitars and tambourines—used melodies half gospel, half country-western, all a little bluesy. And then the preaching. First up was a young man, newly called to the ministry, preaching his heart out and doing a pretty poor job of it. God knows the people tried to help him, feeding him bible texts, urging him on, shouting and speaking in tongues. He gave it all he had, but he could not preach a lick and we all knew it. Finally, in desperation, an old woman in the crowd called out: "Hep him Jesus, hep him." Well, even Jesus couldn't help him preach that day, so the young man sat down deferring to a more seasoned preacher named Brother Byron who began to preach like fury, taking no prisoners. It was hard preaching about sin and salvation, more sin and the promise of deliverance. Suddenly, before I realized what was happening, he walked over to a wooden box with a cross burned into the top, flopped open the lid and lifted up the biggest timber rattler I had ever seen. There he stood, preaching the gospel and wrestling a serpent right before my very eyes. It was amazing, overpowering, and terrifying—everything we Baptists SAY that a worship service is supposed to be, but without the serpents.

"Why do you do it?" I asked my serpent-handling host. He cited the long ending of Mark's gospel—chapter 16, the part not in the earliest manuscripts of the New Testament—then added: "We have to face anybody that comes along." The grammar suffers but the idea intrigues.

Astounded, I recounted the event in my fall church history class at the Baptist Seminary in Louisville where I was then teaching. A couple of months later we were discussing the theology of St. Thomas Aquinas and his five arguments for the existence of God. The ontological argument for God's existence gave the class particular difficulty, and I struggled to get the point across. Finally, in desperation, a student shouted from the back of the room: "Well, hep him, Jesus, hep him." Class dismissed.

I wonder, however, if every class or church gathering should designate someone to call out at the opportune moment, "Hep him, Jesus, hep him!" Why? Because that's what learning is about—wrestling with ideas, good, bad, and ugly, abstract and concrete all at once, some of them as dangerous as serpents.

Jacob knew how to wrestle, didn't he? Indeed, Jacob would wrestle anyone who came along. It all started in the womb. Jacob was a kind of Hulk Hogan/Spider-Man in utero, wrestling with twin brother Esau in their mother's belly before he ever entered the world. Jacob even passed through the birth canal clinging to his brother's heel, a sure sign of things to come. He spent his life wrestling—clawing actually—for his brother's birthright, for his father's blessing,–for the woman named Rachael, even for grace, though it was a long time coming. Do you remember the story?

Jacob, having cheated his brother, conned his father, and used his mother, finds himself alone in the wilderness exiled from family and home, scared Brother Esau will find him and take revenge. But God, not Esau, finds Jacob and claims the best con man this side of Sinai as his own. He dreams of ladders and angels and receives the promise of God's blessing on himself and his descendants. Strange choice, that. You'd think any self-respecting God would give the little liar what he deserved, fry him with judgment right there in the desert. Instead, God chose Jacob, and promises to look out for him. Even self-centered Jacob knows that something significant has happened. "Surely the lord was in this place," he says at Bethel, "and I knew it not." From then on Jacob spars with God, unerringly dense about what it means to be claimed by the divine presence. He makes his way to the home of his uncle Laban who tricks Jacob into fourteen years of work for two marriage licenses. Remember the story? Jacob fell for the lovely Rachael, was told he could wed her after seven years of work for her father, did the work, had the wedding with spouse in the ancient equivalent of the modern chador, and discovered, as the text says poignantly, "in the morning it was Leah," Rachael's older sister. So he worked another seven years for his beloved. Laban's gift as a flimflam man made Jacob look a bit like Mother Teresa. But Jacob survives and finally decides it is time to return to family and home.

In this text, Jacob has gathered up his wives and extended family and headed home with all the baggage of his tawdry past in hand. At the "crossing place" on the river Jabbok, he is forced to confront his past in the person of Esau his brother. "Much afraid and distressed," the text tells us, Jacob prepares to face the brother who has sworn to kill him. Ever the wheeler-dealer, he sends some livestock ahead as a bribe, but he also calls upon God, confessing, "I am not worthy of all the true and steadfast love which thou hast shown to me thy servant." (Gen. 32:10) Apparently Jacob had grown up a bit. *And in the night he wrestles with the stranger who finds him by the river, struggling till daybreak in quest of another blessing.*

It is one of the classic moments of Hebrew history. Jacob wrestles and prevails. But who was that stranger? Theories abound: a night spirit prowling the darkness, brother Esau slipping up on him to settle old scores, or the God who first haunted him in the desert so long before? Or was Jacob simply wrestling with himself, struggling in the darkness with his own shadow side?

Whatever it was, it touched him deeply, threw his hip out of joint and gave him a new name. Suddenly, Jacob the trickster, becomes Israel, meaning "God prevails." Esau too had come of age, it seems, and in the morning they are reconciled, an unbelievable occurrence given the hatred that had festered between them over the years.

Surely the text says this above all: Life is a wrestling match, faith too, for that matter. To live by faith is to wrestle with anything that comes along. Like Jacob, we are ever wrestling with strangers and brothers, sisters and parents, enemies and friends, perhaps with angels, or night spirits, and certainly with ourselves. You never know when you may wind up all alone on some riverbank or in some Godforsaken wilderness with destiny and danger all around, when the things you thought would hold forever fall apart. You never know when the times will take a turn and suddenly you are face-to-face with your deepest fears and darkest doubts. At such moments we had best know how to wrestle, how to struggle until morning, how to hold on to grace.

We religious types often declare that God and gospel will take away all struggles, right all wrongs, reconcile all differences, and end all conflicts. Truth is, faith may get us into more trouble than we bargained for, adding to the complexity of life and relationships. Jacob wrestles at Jabbok and gets a blessing. Jesus wrestles at Gethsemane and gets a cross. Only God knows which way it will go in the morning. Whatever else you learn from this text and a hundred like it, I hope you learned to wrestle, with ideas and issues, moral dilemmas and complex questions.

Who taught you to wrestle with ideas and with yourself? For me, I think it began at students' retreat at the Broadway Baptist Church in Fort Worth, Texas. I was a college freshman, and the retreat was supposed to help us confront certain ethical imperatives, the so-called New Morality of the turbulent 1960s. The speaker was Dr. J. P. Allen, pastor of the Broadway church. He spoke about moral dilemmas, sex, relationships, and faith. When he finished, Dr. Allen asked for questions, and I bounded to my feet full of unlimited adolescent and evangelical zeal, both of which can kill you. "Well," I said, "I find that if we just trust Jesus, and walk with him daily, God will take care of all these moral issues."

Dr. J. P. Allen set his jaw, looked straight into my post-pubescent eyes and responded, "Young man, everything I have said for the last hour was an attempt to avoid that kind of glib, simplistic Christianity." I cannot explain it to you now, but in the complete humiliation of that moment, I began to learn to wrestle—with ideas and with faith, with the inescapable paradoxes of moral, spiritual—indeed, human—life. I can tell you without hesitation, that in that terrible moment I was, quite simply, born again. Humiliation is a painful and poignant teacher that sometimes marks the beginning of real learning.

Who in your life pushed you, challenged you, even humbled you, into wrestling with complexity, wrestling with God and grace? Are there days when you come out of home, hospital room, funeral home, or church with a knot in your stomach or an aching in your head, not because you were rejecting faith, but because faith compelled you to confront something that confused, angered, invigorated, mystified, and terrified you? Perhaps they are struggles you may never resolve, but you will not let them go just yet, for they are too powerful and consuming.

You hold on to them, less because they rob you of faith than that your faith itself will not let them go.

Occasionally, by luck or grace, I was privileged to be present when a student learned to wrestle with history and in so doing came to wrestle with the future as well. Years ago, Kathy Webb took my Church History class, and did a term paper—there is no history without term papers—on St. Francis of Assisi, a most idealistic saint. Later she told me that as Francis heard Christ's word to take the gospel to the poor so did she. She moved into the West End of Louisville, and began living with poor people. She has spent her life doing that, in a variety of out-of-the-way places. For many years she lived with her family in South America wrestling with poverty, hunger, and disease. And it began, in part, because she started wrestling with some stranger through a term paper in a required history class and the life of the most impractical of saints. Alleluia.

Teaching and learning can be sacramental, can't they? Who knows when a word, a paper, a book, or a question may change our lives when we least expect? And when it happens there is nothing like it. Students taught me to wrestle: Earl Marsalis struggling with cancer in unbelievable courage and dignity; Ronald Bobo, seminarian and African-American pastor in the projects, confronting racism in Louisville and drafting me for public demonstrations on a cold day in January; Johnny Young, African-American minister and Wake Forest Divinity graduate, opening his own home to the homeless in Winston-Salem, protesting when the zoning commission ordered him to stop it. Jenny Phillips, one of our daughter's first student sitters who, by the time we returned from the movie, had taught our three-year-old to lift her hands and say, "praise the Lord!" After that, we always asked whether the sitter was charismatic.

Underneath it all, there is conscience. Sooner or later, conscience finds us everyone. Jacob is one of the major cheaters of Hebrew history. Indeed, if I had been God, I would never have chosen the little creep. I would have fried him in the desert and given him what he deserved. Instead, grace prevails and God chooses the conman, blessing him forever.

After all those years of cheating people, Jacob finally learns that some things, even a birthright, aren't worth having at somebody else's expense. At Jabbok something simple and profound occurs before our very eyes. Jacob grows up. He finally takes responsibility for his actions, right or wrong. Conscience clings to us when we know we've done wrong or when we must take a stand—sometimes alone—for what is too deep to relinquish in ourselves and in the faith. It is no easier for us than for Jacob. All our consciences are under siege in the 21st century, caught between moral relativism on one hand and dogmatic totalitarianism on the other. In the end, conscience may be all we have left.

Jesus warned that such things might happen, sending out his earliest followers, instructing them to be wise as serpents, innocent as doves. And then the adds, "And *when* you are arrested," as if he expected it, "do not worry about what to say. God will find a way to say something through you." Wrestling with conscience can be dangerous business.

So the last word in the text is the first word after all: When all is said and done, it is not that we find God, but that God finds us. At Jabbok, Jacob learned that he needed grace and that it had been there all along. The text ends with a brief aside: "and Jacob limped a little from then on." Wrestling strangers and friends is dangerous business. Some of the experiences mark us for life. To live by faith means being broken, bruised, roughed-up considerably, one way or the other. We are "earthen vessels," St. Paul says, objects that chip rather easily in the give and take of daily use (2 Corinthians 4:7). If you want to learn, if you want to live, if you want a blessing, you may get maimed for it. That's just how it is, here or there, then or now—at Jabbok and at Golgotha, in the garden of Gethsemane or up an Appalachian hollow. We are all wrestling something, struggling and hurting, growing old and growing up, conniving and repenting, arrogant and broken, all at once. Chosen, everyone, and desperate for goodness whether we know it or not. Sooner or later, every one of us wrestles with the Eternal Stranger who, as it turns out, will not let us go. Reminding us that even in the darkness, there is grace. Now and forevermore. Amen.

Part III


IN THE DIVINITY SCHOOL:
LECTURES AND ADDRESSES ON THEOLOGICAL
EDUCATION AND CHRISTIAN MINISTRY

# "Not Instruction, but Provocation":
## Doing Theology at a New Divinity School[1]

### Opening Convocation,
### Wake Forest University Divinity School,
### October 1999

It began in controversy. Andover Theological Seminary, the first official theological school in the United States, was founded in 1808 primarily because, as they said, "Harvard went Unitarian." Theological studies began much earlier with undergraduates at Harvard, Yale, and Princeton who, once graduated, then "read theology" with a pastor/mentor in a specific congregation. But Andover was the first of its kind, "the West Point of Orthodoxy," historian Sydney Ahlstrom called it, boasting an "aggressive" faculty, an "enthusiastic" student body, and an evangelical influence that spread like wildfire.[2] If the Unitarians had believed in hell, Andover would have scared it out of them. Anyway, orthodox Andover gained so much ecclesiastical clout that the more liberal folk at Harvard responded by founding a divinity school in 1811. Yale followed in 1822 and the rest is history. From the first, theological seminaries and divinity schools in the U.S. were born of controversy, mirroring the needs and the turmoil of the churches.

Harvard Divinity School was itself a seedbed of debate. In 1838, Ralph Waldo Emerson, part Plato, part Ichabod Crane, attacked the "corpse-cold rationalism" of conservative and liberal alike in his infamous Divinity School address, declaring, as any good Transcendentalist would, that: "Truly speaking, it is not instruction, but provocation, that I can receive from another soul. What he announces, I must find true in me, or reject; and on his word, or as his second, be he

---

[1] This address was given at the Opening Convocation for the founding of the School of Divinity, Wake Forest University, October 1999.

[2] Sydney Ahlstrom, *A Religious History of the American People* (New Haven: Yale University Press, 1972) 394.

who he may, I can accept nothing."[3] For Emerson, truth was not true until perceived from deep within.

On the threshold of a new century, Wake Forest University begins a new divinity school, and the faculty asked me to say what that might mean. Struggling for a "handle" I lighted on Emerson, less for his Transcendentalism, as fascinating as that may be, than for his wonderful imagery. "Not instruction, but provocation": It is a dangerous line and an even more dangerous idea. Provocation, the dictionary says, can be "to incite to anger or resentment," a frightening possibility in any school, and not what we desire here. But it can also mean, "to stir," "to challenge," or "to call forth." So tonight, let us say that, at least in part, this new school seeks to provide, not simply instruction, but provocation that stirs up students, challenging them and calling forth from them ideas and issues that help to form their Christian ministry. Learning is always dangerous and difficult to domesticate. My thesis this evening is this: Sooner or later, all good "instruction" involves "provocation," pressing us beyond our certainty and ourselves, demanding more of us than we ever dreamed possible.

As Emerson's Divinity School Address illustrates, theological provocation is nothing new. We are heirs of noble traditions. In a sense this new divinity school is an effort to provide graduate ministerial education in a university that began in 1834, in part to educate ministers. This audience is filled with friends and colleagues who have invested their lives in theological education through scholarship, struggle, and controversy. Amid our celebration we honor them tonight.

When British Baptists founded what is now Regent's Park College, Oxford, in 1811 they declared "that nothing is farther from our intentions than to interfere with the respectable Seminaries already subsisting, from which the Church of Christ has derived essential benefit.... We are persuaded, however, that the ground is not yet so fully occupied as to leave no room for a further extension of the means of instruction to students in theology." [4] Like those English Baptists, we acknowledge our debt to colleagues in other theological schools. Like such schools, we offer basic instruction toward the Master of Divinity degree with its

---

[3] Ralph Waldo Emerson, "An Address Delivered Before the Senior Class in Divinity College, Cambridge, July 15, 1838," in H. Shelton Smith, Robert T. Handy, Lefferts A. Loetscher, *American Christianity* (Charles Scribner's Sons, 1963) 137.
[4] *Massachusetts Baptist Missionary Magazine*, June 1811, 44.

indomitable core curriculum of Bible, history, theology, pastoral care, spirituality, homiletics, supervised ministry, and mission.

At first glance, all that sounds pretty tame. Even the people who invented that basic curriculum admitted it could be a real snooze. Writing of the courses at the General Theological Seminary in 1856, Episcopal priest and professor Milo Mahan observed:

> Of regular routine work the students have enough: Hebrew, History, Hermeneutics, Systematic Divinity, and the like, are dry and hard studies: and a conscientious teacher, who understands the importance of system, cannot well make them otherwise. Without classroom drill, which is not only hard work, but often somewhat of a bore, no solid foundation can be laid.[5]

Do not be fooled, however. The curriculum of a divinity school is anything but boring. It calls us to struggle with issues that burst out of texts and traditions, spiritual exploration, and pastoral responses. The intensity of these ideas is sometimes beyond measure. And, if the histories of other theological schools suggest anything for Wake Forest University it is this: Open a divinity school and duck! Controversy will strike immediately, if not sooner.

When Cincinnati's Lane Seminary split over abolition in 1835, the anti-slavery students and faculty transferred to the newly formed Oberlin College where abolitionism, revivalism, the holiness movement, and evangelical feminism went hand in hand. Oberlin began with forty-two students, nineteen of whom were female, a scandalous provocation, then and now. It was the world's first coeducational college and the first to permit women to study theology. Antoinette Brown, the first woman ordained in America, graduated Oberlin with a theological degree, as did Lucy Stone, class of 1847. Stone's father refused to fund her education, so she raised the money herself by selling berries. After graduation, when she preached on the lecture circuit, riots broke out.[6]

Sometimes students lead us from instruction to provocation. The Wake Forest University Divinity School, beginning with twenty-four full-time students, nineteen of whom are female, is debtor to Oberlin and other schools whose courageous faculties and students went before us.

---

[5] George Blackman, *Faith and Freedom* (New York: Seabury Press, 1967) 99.

[6] Rosemary Radford Reuther and Rosemary Skinner Keller, *Women and Religion in America*, vol. 3 (San Francisco: Harper & Row, 1986) 251.

They remind us that Christian ministry does not exist in a vacuum. Like them, we are sorting out identities in the midst of changing times.

We say we are "Christian by tradition, ecumenical in outlook, and Baptist in heritage," a confession sure to delight or offend everyone. Some are concerned that we are too ecumenical, others that we are not ecumenical enough. Still others wonder what the word "ecumenical" will mean in a new century. Then there is the dreaded "B-word"— Baptist—a word that strikes fear into the hearts of men, women, and children from coast to coast. Some fear we are too Baptist and others that we are not Baptist enough. I wonder how we shall understand the meaning of that or any denominational heritage in the new century. Some say we are non-denominational, others that we are inter-denominational, and still others that we are post-denominational. One wag suggested we are pan-denominational—we'd support any denomination that panned out for us. I hope we will simply prepare students for ministry in churches now compelled to ask those same questions of themselves.

I also suspect that some of our Wake Forest faculty colleagues may wonder if the term "theological education" is itself paradoxical, if not downright oxymoronic, an attempt to posit education on the premise of God, the Sacred, and other less than objective claims. We have to prove ourselves on this campus.

Likewise, some church-folk still worry that theological education itself may be a detriment to faith, warning our students as people have since 1834, "Don't let them steal your faith up there at Wake Forest." Sam Jones, the Methodist revivalist whose Nashville church housed the first Grand Ole Opry, illustrated that long distrust of seminary education. Commenting in the 1890s, Jones warned: "We have been clamoring for forty years for a learned ministry, and we have got it today and the church is deader than it ever has been in history. Half of the literary preachers in this town are AB's, PhD's, DD's, LLD's and ASS's."[7] Baptists remain suspicious. As an old Baptist once told me: "We don't care much for an educated ministry, we saw what it did to the Presbyterians."

Aware of, but (mostly) undaunted by such concerns, Wake Forest University began plans for a new divinity school more than a decade

---

[7] William G. McLoughlin, Jr., *Modern Revivalism* (New York: Ronald Press, 1959) 288.

ago. Its mission includes the following: First, this is a school of the university, a community of scholars inside a broader community of scholars, providing the perspectives that theological education can bring to scholarship, spirituality, and ethics for and with the university at large. Second, this divinity school prepares ministers for churches. The students in this first class speak of their desire to serve churches as Christian ministers. The forms of that ministry will vary, but most know that they will be involved in preaching, teaching, and counseling, praying with, and guiding congregations or their extended ministries in the church and in the world. Third, the divinity school prepares ministers to respond to basic issues of life and death, pain and struggle, joy and celebration in faith communities where many of the old structures, resources, and identities are in "permanent transition." Fourth, a diverse full-time and adjunct faculty facilitates formation for ministry.

The Divinity School is a strange mix, you must admit. One observer described the faculty as composed of "two feminists, a monk, a controversial expert on religious liberty and two battle-scarred Baptists." The Classics Department is teaching Greek for us; the Religion Department is teaching Hebrew. By next fall we will have an African-American professor of preaching, and a full-time New Testament professor. Two of our Law School colleagues have opened their seminars to our students. Pastoral Care studies are facilitated by the Pastoral Care Center at the Baptist hospital and we are working to raise funds for a chair of Jewish Studies. We hope Professor Maya Angelou will drop by and bless us from time to time. We may even get an Appalachian Mountain preacher to stop in occasionally. Our student body is seventy-five percent female, with a majority who are Baptists of one kind or another. Others are Moravian, Lutheran, Presbyterian, Methodist, and a couple who I'd say "are keeping their denominational options open." Is all this a nightmare of cross-disciplinary diversity and theological correctness? Perhaps. But what if it is the future? Can we draw on the best the university has to offer, all in an effort to prepare ministers for churches learning to draw on multiple resources? In some ways we are very diverse, in other ways hardly diverse at all.

Amid instruction, we will encourage our students to come to terms with pluralism and identity, as well as consensus and dissent, dialectics that confront ministers, churches, and American cultures on the edge of a new millennium.

Religious pluralism seems a given in American society. There are Buddhists in Berea, Kentucky, Hindus in Jacksboro, Texas (population 2,500), and an Islamic Center in downtown Asheville, North Carolina. If folks from those religious traditions have found their way to Berea, Jacksboro, and Asheville, then they are everywhere! Religion classes at this and other universities have become, for many students, occasions for sorting out their religious heritage in families where multiple religious traditions are the norm. They want to know what it means to have family origins that are Protestant/Catholic, Christian/Jewish, Christian/Muslim, Anglo-Saxon/African-American, Anglo-Saxon/Asian, and how all those traditions relate to THEIR quest for faith. Tomorrow's ministers must find ways to respond to these changing religious connections.

Pluralism inside denominations is itself an ecclesiastical given. Many old-line churches now recognize the ordination of ministers in other Christian traditions, permitting pastoral appointment across denominational lines. While ordination inside a specific denomination remains the door to ministry, this generation of ministers may begin in one tradition and move through several others in the course of their careers.

Pluralism leads to many unexpected, "non-traditional" practices. I know Pentecostals who wear clerical collars and elect bishops. I also know some people who refer to themselves as Pentecostal Presbyterians, two words no one ever expected to go together. I know one Alabama pastor who preaches in Reeboks every Sunday. He says he tried Nike but just could not feel the Holy Spirit in them.

Christian pluralism flourishes on this campus. Ten days ago a Jewish filmmaker doing a documentary on Baptists and Jews interviewed me in my office late at night. Suddenly sounds from a student-led service erupted from the Davis Chapel next door. "Are they speaking Hebrew?" the filmmaker asked. "No," I replied, "they are speaking in tongues." This building is full of religious surprises and so is the divinity school student body.

Three years ago, an African-American woman who grew up in Winston-Salem asked me if she were accepted, would she be welcomed for what she could bring to this divinity school. Tonight she sits here as part of our entering class. Three years ago a woman who identifies herself as lesbian asked me whether, if accepted, she would be welcomed for what she would bring to this school. Tonight she sits here as part of our entering class. Last week at a gathering of students another woman expressed thanks for the acceptance and welcome she has received at this new school. She was not sure it would be so since she is different from the other students. She is 74 years old. These three women and their other sister and brother students are welcomed. They are here because of their sense of call, a non-discrimination policy, excellent references, and fine grade point averages. Every one of them is a provocateur extraordinaire. They are shaping this school toward the future through the pluralism of their "voices."

Pluralism challenges us all. This divinity school began the same week that questions regarding gender and same-sex relationships exploded on this campus. As dean of a fledgling school where studying Old Testament, New Testament, and Theology are stressful enough, I'd just as soon those issues would have been delayed awhile. As teacher, historian and Baptist, I know that controversy waits for no one, so we might as well talk about it. Beyond diatribe, beyond accusation, let us listen to all our students and faculty, friends and family, for ultimately these questions are familial and pastoral issues. And, through it all, let us declare again our undying faith in the power of classroom to change our lives. I do not know how to resolve these differences that divide our churches, I just don't, but I know we must not fear to speak about them if we value education and learning.

Amid such pluralism, we ask, what does it mean to claim Christian identity? "Doing theology" means learning to live in multiple worlds, preparing students for ministry in a pluralistic environment while encouraging them in their own search for theological and spiritual identities. For the twenty-first-century minister, pluralism and identity are inseparable. Pluralism challenges us to promote tolerance, work for dialogue, and seek the common good. Identity challenges us to find a place (or places) to stand, from which to reach out, confronting the problems that surround us.

Identity raises questions as old as the church. What does it mean to be Christian? What is the nature of faith? How do we read a text? What is the meaning of baptism and the Supper? How shall churches be governed? What ideas and beliefs are essential and what are *adiaphora*, matters of negotiation?

At first glance finding an identity seems relatively simple. We choose, as Catherine Albanese says, creed, code, cultus, and community and get on with it. But we all know it is much more difficult than that.[8] Denominations are not uniform in belief and practice, religious institutions disappoint, congregations can go sour, and creeds and confessions can be amended often by majority vote. One group's moral absolute is another's moral chaos. Some Christians find identity in dogmas or denominations, others in spirituality or texts, still others in great moral crusades. Many struggle with a combination of all that and more. Nonetheless, we need places to stand, some without ever budging, some negotiating at every turn, theological nomads all the way.

And through it all, we acknowledge that such identities are never uniform. A decade ago I taught church history at a Baptist theological seminary in Fukuoka, Japan. The course spanned two semesters of lectures taught via translator, a wonderful Japanese charismatic Baptist who spoke English as well as he spoke in tongues, thank God. One day, a young woman asked a question I shall never forget. "Sensei," she said, "when the Bible and the mystics talk about losing one's life in the spirit, I realized that I first learned that idea in Buddhism." "Sometimes I can't tell which part of me is Christian and which part of me is Buddhist." "Is that ok?" "Yes," I said, "it is ok." "St. Paul could not always tell which part of him was Jewish and which part was Christian. I sometimes can't tell which part of me is Baptist and which part of me is Southern. Welcome to the club." Her Christian identity was shaped by many influences. For most of us, pluralism and identity get all mixed up together.

In the 21st century, how shall we work together? Where shall we find consensus for cooperative endeavor in clothing the naked, feeding the hungry, liberating the oppressed? Sometimes we can't or don't. The divisions are too deep, the mistrust too severe, and the issues too complex. Divinity schools, old and new, must provoke churches and individuals to search for consensus, community and the common good. Are there things we can do together even as we disagree? Community, like consensus, is elusive. Some find it in the fellowship of great texts, others in specific denominations. Some gravitate to local congregations, others to prayer and support groups. Some "seekers" have been so hurt

---

[8] Catherine L. Albanese, *America: Religions and Religion*, 2nd ed. , (Belmont CA: Wadsworth Publishing, 1992) 10.

by communities—corporate, religious, and familial—that they hesitate to risk.

Consensus and community are troublesome, messy, intrusive, dynamic, sometimes over-rated, and occasionally misused. The same can be said for dissent, but we need them both. Can dissent be taught? Perhaps, at least it can be modeled. Martin Luther King, Jr., learned the rubrics of dissent in the black church, in ethics classes at Boston University, and in reading M. K. Gandhi. But it was as a Baptist preacher in Montgomery, Alabama, that he confronted events that took him where he never expected to go.

Dorothy Day, mystic, long-time social activist and founder of the Catholic Worker Movement, learned that dissent did not come easily. She wrote:

> Certainly the first time I went to jail—when I was eighteen—I felt a great sense of desolation, a great identification with all the hopeless people around me. I didn't have the faith. I spent a couple of days weeping and I just went into a state of melancholy. I never feel unsure in prison anymore.... I think I'm absolutely sure of these things—the works of mercy and the nonviolent rebuilding of the social order. I think there has to be a sort of harmony of body and soul, and I think that comes about, certainly for a woman, through those very...simple things of "feeding the hungry, clothing the naked, and sheltering the harborless."[9]

Dorothy Day was a social—though not a theological—dissenter, never really questioning the Catholic tradition to which she converted with the first pangs of morning sickness. Dissenters learn to choose their battles.

Some dissent is "over-against." It is Elijah shaking a boney finger in the establishment's face and declaring: "Choose you this day whom you shall serve." Some dissent is inside out. Jesus called it leaven, slowly "provoking" a lump of dough into action. Either way there is an explosion.

If you intend to be a lifetime prophet, best to work out a permanent relationship with U-Haul. You will be packing the trailer with regularity, and moving on down the road. Dissent is risky and exciting, but, as Baptist preacher Carlyle Marney reminded us, priestliness and the prophetic

---

[9] *New Yorker* (9 August 1999): 53–4.

are inseparable. Marney warned: "It is in the alleys where one 'priests' that one arrives at credentials for an occasional prophetic moment."[10]

Thus "doing theology" in a divinity school ultimately requires asking what such studies mean for ministry in the churches. Ultimately, we must hope that all this research and learning may provoke us to greater understanding of what the ancients called "the care of souls."

In summer 1988, I taught in the Appalachian Ministries Educational Resource Center in Berea, Kentucky, and certain female students decided to interview a woman holiness preacher as part of their research project. They found Sister Lydia Surgener, owner of a used-clothing store in Pennington Gap, Virginia, and preacher at a little church up a holler from Cranks Creek, Kentucky.[11] When Sister Liddy discovered it, the church was boarded up and seemed dead as a doornail, but, she said, "That church isn't dead, it's just asleep." She believed that God told her to wake it up. She and her nephew, Junior, went there each Sunday and Sister Liddy would preach and Junior would sing, just the two of them. Gradually, some people started coming, and last I heard it was a flourishing congregation.

"Doing theology," in this or any school means instructing, indeed, provoking generations of ministers who will "wake up" some churches, "catch up" with others, and perhaps tell some it's time to take a little nap. It is declaring, with Sister Liddy, "This church isn't dead, it's just asleep."

As he began his own ministry, Jesus woke up some folks in his hometown with words from the prophet Isaiah that send us forth tonight. "The Spirit of the Lord is upon me," he said, "anointing me to announce good news to the poor, To proclaim release for prisoners and recovery of sight for the blind; To let the broken victims go free, To proclaim the year of the Lord's favour." (Luke 4:18)

Do you hear the provocation in those words? And the hope? Amen.

---

[10] Carlyle Marney, "Sermon at the Ordination of Bruce Curry Page," audiotape in the author's possession.
[11] Deborah Vansau McCauley, *Appalachian Mountain Religion: A History* (Urbana: University of Illinois Press, 1995) 59–61, describes the ministry of Sister Lydia Surgener.

# After the Rains Come

## Dean's Lunch for New Students,
## Wake Forest University School of Divinity,
## August 2000

It was spring in Israel—last spring (2000), to be exact. The rains had been unseasonably prolific, and we were roaming around that Holy Land. Flowers were everywhere, and all those Bible verses came roaring back

"For lo the winter is past, the rains are over and gone, flowers appear on the earth, the time for the singing of birds has come." (Song of Sgs 2:11)

"In days to come Jacob shall take root, Israel shall blossom and put forth shoots, and fill the whole world with fruit." (Isa. 27:6)

"The wilderness and the dry land shall be glad, the desert shall rejoice and blossom; like the crocus it shall blossom abundantly, and rejoice with joy and singing!" (Isa. 35:1–2)

All that happened, right before my very eyes. Crocus, jasmine, lavender blossoms galore erupted out of every crevice and meadow. It was exactly like the words of the Hebrew Bible. That week, moderns and postmoderns, religious and non-religious, Jew and Palestinian poured out of Jerusalem and into the countryside to watch the flowers bloom in the wilderness. At Caesarea Philippi flowers were everywhere, often hanging precariously from the rocks and hillsides. Was it like that the day that Jesus of Nazareth took his disciples on retreat to the headwaters of the Jordan? Did the followers of the Greek god Pan, whose temple was at Caesarea Philippi, also see the flowers pushing from the rocky hillside above the Jordan?

Seeing all that, I remembered the Hebrew word: *mitbar*, which we translate as desert or wilderness. It is an Exodus word: "And Moses tended the flock in the backside of the desert." (Exod. 3:1–5) You see, *mitbar* literally means, "to bring the flock to pasture." One scholar says it this way: "During the rainy season and shortly after, the shepherds have their flocks graze in arid and semiarid regions that are not suitable for permanent residence."[1]

May I say it another way? Perhaps the desert, the wilderness is best described as, "Where you take the flocks after the rains come." When the rains come, and the wilderness blooms, we venture into places we have not been before.

So here is my thesis with you on this day of beginnings: Perhaps a divinity school, perhaps this divinity school, can be understood as something like a desert—a wilderness—a place "where you take the flocks after the rains come." It is not a place where you can stay forever, nor is it always a "sacred" place.

Like the desert/wilderness, divinity school is not a place everyone chooses to come. In fact, most people in the real world don't choose to do this, and many wonder why in the world *you* would. It is a place where there is sustenance and challenge, security and insecurity, danger and sanctuary.

Think of all the people who have gone to the desert/wilderness for theological/spiritual education.

Moses, in the backside of the desert, confronts the burning bush—hierophany, we say, in religious studies—God revealed in the ordinary. There he learns that he is called, that he is broken, that he has a mission, and that God can find him in the unexpected places.

The Israelites wandered forty years in the *mitbar*—Let us pray that none of you take that long to finish the Master of Divinity degree!

John the Baptizer comes, dare we say it, out of the wilderness, with a wilderness diet and a death-defying rhetoric.

Jesus goes into the wilderness for forty days and nights to be tempted by the devil, wrestling with himself, as well as with the tempter.

Paul spends three years in the desert of Arabia—just the length of a Master of Divinity degree—with unspeakable encounters with the Divine, he says.

Many of the early Christians—we call them desert fathers and mothers—fled to the wilderness to escape the corruption of the city and find themselves in the search for God.

The earliest settlers to America were convinced that this was a wilderness where they would learn of God as no other people had done

---

[1] Leslie J. Hoppe, *A Guide to the Lands of the Bible* (Collegeville MN: Liturgical Press, 1999) 131.

since Israel. The Quakers, for example, called wilderness Pennsylvania a "Holy Experiment." The Puritans, when they weren't hanging Quakers, called Massachusetts in John Winthrop's words of 1630, a "Citty upon a Hill," noting with a bit of over speak: "The eies (eyes) of all people are upon us."[2] Roger Williams, the quintessential colonial dissenter and occasional Baptist, invented Rhode Island and in so doing invented religious America, with the wonderful line: "I desired it might be a shelter for persons distressed of conscience."[3] I love that phrase. Indeed, it often sustains me. In the Rhode Island wilderness Williams created shelter for persons distressed of conscience. I hope we do, too, here at Wake Forest University.

So today I commend divinity school, this divinity school, to you as wilderness. Today, with you, the class that joins us in our second year, I want to suggest that perhaps your divinity school experience is a bit like a sojourn in that sometime-arid region, "where you take the flocks after the rains come." Will you let me press this metaphor with you a bit today, mindful of Kathleen Norris's insight that we sometimes focus "on the fuzzy boundaries, where definitions give way to metaphor"?[4] At divinity school, when the boundaries get a bit "fuzzy," the metaphor of wilderness may help us understand what we are about.

Both the wilderness and the divinity school are dangerous places. As Leslie Hoppe comments: "The desert then is an out-of-the-way place. It is not where people normally live because it is...dangerous."[5] In the *mitbar* the flock and the pilgrim are at the mercy of predators—animal and human (and we might add, spiritual and theological, ethical, and pastoral). The wilderness is intense; it is where one confronts the forces of darkness, faces the deep questions of life and death, and struggles with calling and vocation. It is where individuals strive to come to terms with God and themselves. Hoppe notes that in Hebrew history, at least at certain points, "the wilderness is not presented as a goal but as a *rite of*

---

[2] John Winthrop, *A Model of Christian Charity, 1630*, in H. Shelton Smith, Robert T. Handy, and Lefferts A. Loetscher, eds., *American Christianity*, vol. 1 (New York: Charles Scribner's Sons, 1960) 102.

[3] Roger Williams, Deed, 1661, cited in the introduction to Williams, *The Bloudy Tenent of Persecution for the Cause of Conscience Discussed*, ed. Edward Bean Underhill (London: J. Haddon, 1848) xxv.

[4] Kathleen Norris, *The Cloister Walk* (New York: Riverhead Books, 1987) 58.

[5] Hoppe *A Guide to the Lands of the Bible*, 131.

*passage* into the Promised Land."[6] Moses says it this way when confronting the burning bush: "Let us *come aside*" and see what God is doing. To confront God is dangerous, awesome, compelling, transforming, painful, and disturbing. The wilderness may bloom, but it is always full of danger.

While the wilderness is a place of escape, it is not for the escapists. Time in the wilderness prepares us to confront the world, and that also is dangerous. In a work entitled, *The Word in the Desert*, Douglas Burton-Christie writes of the men and women in the early church who sought the wilderness:

> They audaciously battled the demons in the desert, but humbly refused to acknowledge their own power. They spoke words of authority, though it was often in their silence that they were most eloquent. Many…refused to participate in the growing establishment of the church under Constantine, choosing instead to live on the margins of society under the direct guidance of the Spirit and the Word of God. Yet in spite of or perhaps because of their singular response to the issues of their time, they had a far-reaching impact on contemporary society and church and left a rich and varied legacy.[7]

Might we do that? Here we talk about God, about faith, about belief, and we wade into the text of the Bible; we bring together our multiple traditions, and we make ourselves vulnerable, unbelievably vulnerable, to each other about some of life's deepest ideas, hopes, and identities. We sojourn in the wilderness to prepare ourselves to confront the dangers found in the many cities of humanity, polluted, hurting, and overflowing with human need.

Calling is dangerous enough, isn't it? What brought you here? Visions, voices, and ecstasies like the medieval mystics or frontier revivalists? Years of struggle with, for, against a calling you are still trying to understand? Or simply a sense that this was something you had to do, had to try, before you went further in this life or the next?

And what about those ideas that brought you here? Ideas are dangerous and disturbing, and this is a place where we struggle with ideas. Ideas challenge us to come to terms with our own beliefs and

---

[6] Ibid, 132.
[7] Douglas Burton-Christie, *The Word in the Desert* (New York: Oxford University Press, 1993), 3.

practices, to ask why we believe what we believe and why we practice what we practice.

All of us live out of doctrines, traditions, scripture, and conscience—among other things—all mixed in together. The danger is that we think our set of formulae, approaches, and non-negotiables are the only ones available.

Wilderness is a place of testing and so is divinity school, both literally and figuratively. We test you here, in your heads, in your hearts, and, alas, on paper. All that makes you exceedingly vulnerable to your teachers and to each other. I remember, years ago, a student of mine received a D-plus on an examination. He wrote me a note saying, "The catalogue says that a D is "poor." Does a D-plus this mean I'm poor, but I'm really good at it?" You will be tested here, in more ways than you can imagine. Together, we are always sorting out what those tests mean.

Wilderness is a place of confrontation—we confront each other here sometimes gently, sometimes boldly, occasionally inappropriately. Indeed, one of the great challenges is to discover ways to confront each other with ideas, while respecting each other as fellow pilgrims.

When confronting the dangers of ideas, the easiest way out is to shoot the messenger. Shooting the messenger simply stalls our own need to deal with the issues at hand. I say that for my own self-protection and hope a word to the sufficient is wise.

Another way of dealing with dangerous ideas is to attack the character of the person who represents them. That still keeps us from confronting the danger as it comes to us.

The wilderness is dangerous because there the pilgrim confronts the darkness, the loneliness, and the vulnerable places of life and faith.

Divinity school is a scary place; let's own that from day one. It will push you, stretch you, enrage you, exhaust you, and force you into the dangerous places of Christian and human life and thought. But, you will have to confront those dangers in the church, and you might as well do it before you get out there with the folks.

And, it's not nearly as dangerous as it has been in the past. Think about it. We are the last divinity school of the twentieth century. But sixty years before in Nazi-infested Germany Dietrich Bonhoeffer helped to start a seminary, an underground seminary. Imagine sneaking by dark of night to a "moveable" divinity school, one lecture ahead of the Brown Shirts. Imagine choosing to study at a time and place that meant arrest,

---

and, as Bonhoeffer himself showed, death. On 17 August 1943 he wrote in his prison journal of his grief over "the death of the three young pastors" who had studied with him at one of the underground seminaries in Finkenwalde: "Of all my pupils, those three were closest to me. It is a great loss, both for me personally and for the Church. More than thirty of my pupils have fallen by now, and most of them were among my best..."[8] Today we can only imagine what it was like to decide to go to divinity school at a time, in a country, when persecution, war, and imprisonment were certain realities.

In those difficult times, Bonhoeffer pushed his students to learn, to think, to struggle, and to challenge the prevailing theological systems of their time, but he also called them to remember the foundations of their search. He wrote, in words that continue to press us, frighten us, and challenge us: "Only the (one) whose final standard is not his reason, his principles, his conscience, his freedom, or his virtue, but who is ready to sacrifice all this when...called to obedient and responsible action in faith and in exclusive allegiance to God—the responsible (one), who tries to make (a) whole life an answer to the question and call of God. Where are these responsible people?" Perhaps that is the greatest danger in this, or any wilderness, confronting the presence, the question and the call of God.

Wilderness is dangerous, but it is also sanctuary. It is where we go to seek safety and space to explore the world and our inner selves. The wilderness is both a frightening place and a place of safety. Leslie Hoppe says that the people who lived in the ancient desert community of Qumran, "went there to be safe from the attacks of the 'wicked priests' and the 'sons of darkness' who ruled Jerusalem," who ruled the city. God, they believed, would drive out the evil ones and restore the good community. They "saw the desert as a place of transition and preparation."[9] Transition and preparation, now those are two words that should shape your understanding of why you are here and what we are doing together.

Thomas Merton, the great twentieth-century Catholic monk and writer, noted the desert fathers and mothers:

---

[8] Dietrich Bonhoeffer, *Letters and papers from Prison* (New York: The Macmillan Company, 1967), 43.
[9] Leslie J. Hoppe, *A Guide to the Lands of the Bible*, 132.

What they sought most of all was their own true self, in Christ. And in order to do this, they had to reject completely the false, formal self, fabricated under social compulsion in "the world." They sought a way to God that was uncharted and freely chosen, not inherited from others who had mapped it out beforehand. They sought a God whom they alone could find, not one who was "given" in a set, stereotyped form by somebody else.[10]

Then he added: "Obviously such a path could only be traveled by one who was alert and very sensitive to the landmarks of a trackless wilderness."[11]

In this wilderness, you can also struggle with the question of "why"—why you are here, why you have "come aside," and where you will go when you leave us. Some speak of the "why" as a "calling." Others eschew such a designation and simply do what they must. Jesus calls disciples by the Sea of Galilee, but he also tells a story of those who simply put their hands to the plow and do not look back.

In a new book called *The Close: A Young Woman's First Year at Seminary*, Chloe Beyer, daughter of the Supreme Court justice, writes:

When seminarians address the "Why" question, we are not merely describing how we wound up in this line of work. We have the privilege and responsibility of explaining our daily vocational tasks, our relationship to the church and our views of it as an institution, and our personal beliefs about what gives life meaning. Indeed, addressing the question "Why?" is a daunting task. Not having a rule of life so intimately related to their professional responsibilities, doctors or hairdressers don't face this peculiar challenge. The story that really "connects the dots" for each seminarian requires effort.[12]

At our best, I hope this divinity school will be a safe place—a place where persons are accepted, heard, and affirmed. I hope this is a place where you can ask all the questions welling up in you, and some you do not yet know you need to ask. Good teaching not only answers our questions, it helps us formulate better ones. I hope it will be a place where you can connect some, but certainly not all, the dots.

---

[10] Thomas Merton, "The Wisdom of the Desert," in *The Thomas Merton Reader*, (Garden City NY: Image Books, 1974) 476.

[11] Ibid., 477.

[12] Chloe Beyer, *The Close: A Young Woman's First Year at Seminary* (New York: Basic Books, 2000) xii.

So as you enter this safe yet dangerous place, here are some realities of the terrain:

This is a Divinity School of the University—We hope to connect to the broader university community in graduate courses, adjunct professors, special events, and diverse interaction.

We are a community at worship, gathering every Tuesday for services planned by faculty and students.

We are a graduate school, committed to representing graduate education as rigorous, dynamic, and challenging as any of the other schools of the university, law, management, medicine, and graduate liberal arts.

You will find many courses difficult and will have to work very hard.

If you have questions, difficulties, special needs or other concerns, see your professors sooner rather than later. We are here to help, and we do not read minds.

This is an academic community, not a church. While we work hard to be a churchly community, we are not a church. We are committed to the church, preparing ministers for the church, and worshiping in a variety of churches, but our primary calling is distinct from the church. We are a community, an academic community of teachers and students, learners everyone.

This is a new divinity school, so we are ever learning, shaping, reshaping, and renewing our work as we seek to make this the best possible school. You help us do that. In a sense, we are all laborers together in the process of shaping this new endeavor. Welcome to that process. You can make this *mitbar* blossom, "For see, the winter is past! The rains are over and gone; the flowers appear in the countryside; the season of birdsong has come."[13] Honest it has. Amen.

---

[13] Song of Songs 2:11–12 *Revised English Bible.*

# Ministry in a "Mixed" World

## Dean's Address,
## Wake Forest University Divinity School,
## August 2004

My God, you should hear the Welsh sing! At least the ones I heard on a Sunday night in July 2004 at the Orchard Hills Baptist Church in Neath, Wales, where my friend Dr. Karen Smith is pastor. I went with a group of nine students and friends of the WFU Divinity School to the evening service where, as one of the members said, "We sing the old hymns." And did they ever! Some fifty or sixty of the older members showed up to hear Karen's superb sermon and to sing their hearts out. The sound and hope of their voices haunts me yet. At every hymn I could not decide whether to sing, to listen, or to weep; so I did a little bit of everything.

It was Bonhoeffer's song that undid me completely. Dietrich Bonhoeffer, the German theologian/martyr wrote the hymn in January 1945, only months before he died at the hands of the Nazis. Its poignant verses include these words offered to God:

> If once again, in this *mixed world,* you give us;
> The joy we had, the brightness of your sun,
> We shall recall what we have learned through sorrow;
> And dedicate our lives to you alone.[1]

From a German prison, to a Welsh church, to the beginning of a new divinity school year, we taste the reality of those words. The world God has given us is a *mixed world,* where things are often bright and dark; struggle and victory; good and evil all at once, where the same sun that rises over our pristine quad, looks down on yet another car bombing in Baghdad. It has been that way, our forbears said, since Adam and Eve

---

[1] Dietrich Bonhoeffer, "By Gracious Powers," in *Baptist Praise and Worship* (Oxford UK: Oxford University Press, 1991) 175.

set out east of Eden in a new, mixed world, ever exhilarating and unceasingly dangerous. We often say that Christians are to be "in the world, but not of it," not knowing, most of us, what in the hell (or heavens) that phrase means.

And here you are, setting your faces toward three years of theological education, already aware, I suspect, that the world is a mixed place indeed. So, charged with the duty of addressing your future here at Wake Forest University, I would make the following observations, punctuated for me this summer by various Christian brothers and sisters during three weeks in London.

First, let us say that a relentless globalism compels us to find new ways to work together across God's world. We reach out to other communities of faith at home and abroad because there is so much to be done in feeding the hungry, clothing the naked, enabling the disabled, preaching the word, that we cannot do it alone. While this assertion is nothing new, it came home to me profoundly this summer in meetings with folks in London.

On the first Wednesday in July (2004) I attended the monthly breakfast meeting of the central London ministers' coalition, a gathering of individuals, Protestant and Catholic, male and female from a wide spectrum of churches and theologies in the inner city. It was a mini-graduate seminar for me as they spoke about their ministries individually and collectively. Every one of their diverse traditions is experiencing a shortage of ministers, particularly individuals age thirty-five and younger. They work in a country where the average church attendance is around 7 percent and in a city where it is probably lower than that. Many of their churches are struggling to find funds that enable them to do ministry and repair their old, often historic, buildings. Indeed, near the end of the meeting, the rector of the historic St. Martins-in-the-Fields Church whose sanctuary rises up from the edge of Trafalgar Square, asked: "We are so diverse, what in the world holds us together?" To which one of the women ministers responded: "Perhaps it is scaffolding."

It is more than that, of course. Theirs is the recognition that the world is changing very quickly inside and outside the church and that in one particular urban segment of that world, the people of God need each other as never before. Some of the ministers spoke of the diversity and transitions within their own ranks. One Anglican minister told of two ordinations he had attended earlier in the summer. One was elaborately high church with full vestments, incense, and extensive use of ancient rites. The other was a three-hour, charismatic-oriented service packed to the rafters with young people, many of whom spoke in tongues at various segments of the service. Both individuals were ordained for the Anglican Church!

Others spoke about the growing influence of so-called "immigrant churches" in London, the source of most of the numerical increases for Anglicans and Baptists alike, congregations much more charismatic and conservative than the standard British churches, realities that create spiritual energy and theological controversy literally right and left. Still others reflected on the impact of the "new spirituality" on the churches and the increasing need to cooperate with non-Christian religious groups—Muslims and Buddhists, for example—in the use of space and a response to human needs in the inner city. When people are starving, homeless, or sick you don't ask their religion before you care for them.

Cooperation does occur. One Catholic priest at St. Ann's church in the infamous SoHo district of London said his little congregation decided to stage its own "parade" in this very secular environment so they began to carry the Blessed Sacrament out into the streets to remind citizens of Christ's presence in the midst of pubs, sex shops and triple-X movie theatres. And the nearby Pentecostal congregation has joined them in the parade! Catholics and Pentecostals in common witness on the streets of SoHo.

Geoff Cornell, a new minister friend, told of cooperative efforts in responding to homelessness through the Hinde Street Methodist Church in central London. Here, Christians from multiple denominations work together to get people off the streets and lobby the government to provide rehabilitation efforts that keep them off the streets.

After these and other encounters with London Christians, my sense is that these urban Christians are something of a ministerial avant-garde. That is, they are ahead of many of us in confronting the realities of a burgeoning secularism, urbanism, globalism, and, frankly, ministerial shortage. These issues have been with us for years, but they are intensifying at breakneck speed.

Knowing that, we must prepare you accordingly. And this is why the Urban Ministry Centre at WFU Divinity School, directed by Professor Doug Bailey is so important to us and to a growing constituency in cities around the country. Likewise, Geoff Cornell at Hinde Street Methodist Church, and Brian Haymes, minister of Bloomsbury Central Baptist Church, want to work with us in developing internships for WFU students who might live in London one or two semesters and work with them in cooperative ministry. Ryan Parker, a divinity school senior, did that last spring, to rave reviews from the Bloomsbury membership. In this *mixed world* we must be intentional about cooperation, community, and relationships that foster ministry together. Globalism must find its way into all our classes, however.[2]

Second, in this *mixed world*, ideas still matter and divide us incessantly. Ideas and actions in this election year have split our nation almost down the middle between what the media calls the "red" and the "blue" states. Indeed, one pundit recently remarked that the country is so split that the presidency may be decided by six people in Ohio! Recent primary elections in our own region give evidence of the way in which Christianity is up for grabs as a campaign tool.

Ideas matter in the church as well. As an historian I am continually struck by the way in which ancient ideas continue to galvanize religious individuals who never heard of the Council of Nicaea, the Marburg Colloquy, or the Clarendon Code, but are deeply galvanized, even divided this very day, by the ideas they represent. In a world where racial, ethnic, and religious intermarriage is increasingly normative, it is best to know all you can about your own and somebody else's cultural and theological baggage if you are going to minister—indeed, communicate—at all.

And in your first week of divinity school we would do well to remind you of this: We don't simply live in a *mixed world*; we also live in a *mixed church*. Many Christians are unable or unwilling to cooperate because of the ideas and dogmas that divide them irrevocably. Cooperation becomes impossible because convictions cannot be bridged. In the church, sorting the negotiable from the non-negotiable is complex and messy. As Martin Luther is alleged to have said, the Church of Jesus Christ is like the ark of Noah. Were it not for the storm without, we could not endure the stench within!

At another conference in London the first week in August, I listened to Dr. Toivo Pilli, a young Estonian scholar, tell of the joys and struggles

---

[2] In 2011 there are two other students from Wake Forest University School of Divinity who have done internships at Bloomsbury Central Baptist Church.

of trying to develop cooperation between Protestants in Eastern Europe after the fall of the Soviet Union and the need to bring together ministerial students to talk about common global mission. Yet many of those churches cannot talk about ministry because of their divisions over the role of women. Some come from communions in which women are ordained and active in public ministry and some where women must essentially remain silent in the churches, sitting in their own segregated area of the church at worship. He also spoke of the new religious establishments developing in many eastern countries where Orthodox churches are reasserting prerogatives lost in Soviet days and now reclaimed at the expense of other Protestant communities.

So here you are in a school and a world where we must come to terms with ideas, acknowledge our differences and struggle to find ways to communicate together. Here at WFU we are a microcosm of the *mixed world*. Some of us will never agree on certain essentials of theology and practice, but can we learn to disagree without attacking the character of those who differ from us? Can we find ways to worship, minister, pray, and study together, all the while listening and learning from each other and retaining those convictions that are at the center of our being? We might as well try to learn those things here, if we want to attempt such radical community out there in the church and the world.

Finally, given these realities, in this *mixed world* we go looking for ways to nurture conscience and dissent, cooperating in ministry while facilitating "voice" for everyone. Pluralism and questions of voice are at the heart of our postmodern future. This reality came home visually to me each morning the first week in August when I ran with a German and an Alabamian along the Thames River in the Chelsea section of the city. On one side of the river is a wonderful statue of Sir Thomas More, humanist scholar, author of the classic work, *Utopia,* and Lord Chancellor of England under Henry VIII. In good conscience, as a committed Catholic, More would not support Henry's decision to break with Rome and declare himself "Supreme Head of the Church on Earth in England." Because more would not conform, he was executed on Tower Hill in 1535, one of the great Catholic martyrs of the Reformation. But just across the River Thames in Battersea Park is another statue, indeed, four statues of the Buddha, cast into a beautiful shrine/stupa that contains a relic from that Indian holy man. The presence of those shrines reflects pluralism that neither Thomas More nor Henry VIII would have imagined, or appreciated. More and Buddha gaze across the river at each other, monuments to old religions and new pluralism, each reflecting the power of conscience, one against a new Reformation and the other against an old Hinduism.

Nurturing conscience amid inevitable pluralism is a challenge we must take seriously with you in this divinity school. I hope we can anticipate that challenge as creatively as those individuals who created the colony of Rhode Island with insights few other colonial citizens of the so-called New World bothered to contemplate.

Baptist leader Dr. John Clarke, with Roger Williams the founder of the colony of Rhode Island, insisted that: "No such believer, or Servant of Christ Jesus hath any liberty, much less Authority, from his Lord, to smite his fellow servant, nor yet with outward force, or arme of flesh, to constrain, or restrain his Conscience, no nor yet his outward man for Conscience sake."[3] Together Clarke and Williams wrote conscience and pluralism into the charter of Rhode Island, noting,

> No person within said Colony, at any time hereafter, shall be in any wise molested, punished, disquieted, or called in question for any differences of opinion in matters of religion, …but that all and any persons may, from time to time, and at all times hereafter, freely and fully have and enjoy his and their own judgments and consciences in matters of religious concernments throughout the tract of land hereafter mentioned.[4]

Now I call that a real "Patriot Act." In our own *mixed world*, polarized and divided, can we defend conscience and pluralism as bravely as they? Help us do that here, if you dare!

So here you are, living in this fourth year of the twenty-first century in a *mixed world*, a *mixed church*, and, for the next three years, in a *mixed divinity school*. We are at once organized and messy; collegial and confrontational; scholarly and pragmatic; spiritual and worldly, diverse and uniform, with miles to go before any of us sleep, and with plenty of improvement necessary in each new day. Help us deal with those realities for the next three years and beyond. And we will be the better for it.

---

[3] H. Shelton Smith, Robert T. Handy, and Lefferts A. Loetscher, *American Christianity*, 2 vols. (New York: Scribner, 1960–63) 1:168; and Bill J. Leonard, *Baptist Ways: A History* (Valley Forge: Judson Press, 2003) 77.

[4] O. K. Armstrong and Marjorie Armstrong, *The Baptists in America* (Garden City NJ: Doubleday, 1979) 71.

God alone knows what lies ahead for the church and the world. Given that we are all mortal, it is entirely possible that something unexpected may descend on any of us at any moment. When I gave an address such as this in August of 2001, I never imagined that less barely two weeks later, on September 11, all hell would break lose in our country and around the world. But when we joined with 800 students for an impromptu communion service on that fateful afternoon, we clung to one another and to hope. We still do. And Dietrich Bonhoeffer's words from prison still bring courage for the days ahead:

And when the cup God gives is filled to brimming,
With bitter suffering, hard to understand.
We take it gladly, trusting through the trembling,
Out of so good and so beloved a hand.[5]

Welcome to the Divinity School at Wake Forest University. Expect the unexpected, and be glad. Amen.

---

[5] Bonhoeffer, "By Gracious Powers," 175.

# Out on a Limb? Not Yet!

## Dean's Luncheon,
## Wake Forest University Divinity School,
## August 2005

On 7 July 2005, terrorists blew up three subway trains and a city bus in downtown London. More than fifty people were killed. And you came to divinity school.

In the spring of 2005, Pope John Paul II died and was buried in one of the great medieval spectacles of the new twenty-first century. Millions of people went to Rome. And you came to divinity school.

In July 2005, Joel Osteen led his 40,000-member congregation at Lakewood Church, Houston, into their new quarters at the Compaq Center, a former basketball arena, which they promptly packed out with more than 20,000 people attending each service. Joel's never been to divinity school, but you've decided to give it a shot!

In August 2005, more than 1,850 American soldiers have been killed in Iraq, and only God knows how many Iraqis. And you came to divinity school.

In August 2005, the mother of a 22-year-old soldier killed in Iraq decided to camp out in front of the Texas White House outside Crawford, Texas in hopes of an audience with the President of the United States in order to urge that he brings the troops home. And you came to divinity school.

In her *New York Times* column for 10 August 2005, commenting on that mother in that place, Maureen Dowd wrote that "the moral authority of parents who bury children killed in Iraq is absolute."[1] Can *you* exegete that haunting phrase or any of these events I've just described? Can you offer "an explanation or interpretation" for a medieval and a postmodern spectacle, both drawing huge numbers of people in the year of our Lord 2005? Can you exegete—offer an explanatory note—biblical, historical, theological, spiritual, pastoral, that

---

[1] Maureen Dowd, *New York Times*, 10 August 2005.

says anything to a mother or father whose twenty-something son or daughter was snuffed out by a roadside bomb or suicide bomber? After a week, a semester, or three years in this divinity school will your exegesis of these texts and contexts be the same as one you'd offer right now?

This Master of Divinity program that you are beginning does many things, but one central issue is surely centered in this important question: Can you exegete texts and contexts past, present, and future? Can you dig into the texts, the sources, the resources and struggle with the ideas that have engaged and divided religious communions from Canaan to Constantinople, from Syria to Saddleback Valley? Actually, we are less interested here in your opinion of these and other events, than we are in your ability to *document* that opinion, or build a case for it, or struggle with ancient ideas and primary sources that might in-form or re-form your opinion and analysis. In coming to terms with those sources and resources you will make yourselves very vulnerable to us as faculty, and also to each other, and to the sources themselves, both ancient and modern. In short, I suppose, we could say that you get out on a limb.

Vulnerability is at the heart of our communal experience here at the Wake Forest University Divinity School. Every graduate program requires certain vulnerability from its students as they face examinations, papers, class discussions, and other evaluatory experiences. But at divinity school we add God, faith, dogma, doctrine, tradition, dissent, spirituality, and doubt to the mix. Was it Martin Luther who reminded us that one becomes a theologian by "living, dying and being damned?" (And that's just in the first semester!) Yes, you are out on a limb here. There will be classes in which you wish you hadn't said what you said out loud and other classes where you wish you'd said something, anything, just to let people know you are thinking about these issues even when you aren't sure where they will take you. Yes, you are out on a limb, gambling that you can do this degree in three years apart from illness, family crisis, personal angst, and economics, economics, economics. What we hope and encourage you to do is to take advantage of the university infrastructure—student insurance, writing center, counseling center, basketball tickets—that will undergird your pilgrimage here amid the vulnerabilities.

But in a much larger sense, during the next three years you are hardly out on a limb at all. Indeed, our hope for you is that this academic program and this community of pilgrims will serve as an anchor, a foundation, or a tree trunk, not a limb. For it is out there, in the world, in the thick of things that we are most vulnerable, most out on a limb as women and men "for others." Some of you will move from this degree to a church were you will crawl up into a pulpit at least forty-five or more Sundays a year, climb down into a text taken from the lectionary or the sermon roulette process we Baptists often manifest, take your clothes off (theologically and homiletically speaking) in front of a group of people, and make yourself exceedingly vulnerable to differences of opinion, ethical division, theological dispute, and perhaps even charges of heresy before it is done! That's life on an ecclesiastical limb. We've got to help get you ready for that.

Or you'll find yourself in the emergency room at 2 a.m. when somebody's teenager has wrapped a car and perhaps themselves around a bridge or a lamppost and they need somebody, anybody, to help them deal with life's, and perhaps death's, unexpected turns. Can we do anything here that helps anchor you even slightly at that unpredictable moment? Or can you deal with the homeless and the city council in your particular locale in the name of justice and goodness and God? We'll hope to get you ready for that.

You've got plenty of company among that "cloud of witnesses" that went ahead of us. These days I think often about Ann Hasseltine, an early nineteenth-century woman who as a young woman attended Branford Academy, a "finishing school" for young women, as she couldn't go to Harvard, Yale, or Princeton. While there she read Jonathan Edwards's monumental work not yet a century in print entitled *The History of the Work of Redemption*. Caught up in that work she decided that she should go out as part of the fledgling missionary movement invigorating her generation of young Christians. But she was a woman, and churches weren't sending out women on these global endeavors. So she looked around for a husband who was on the same theological page and found Adoniram Judson, a recent graduate of Williams College.

The two went out to India in 1812, sent by the American Board of Commissioners for Foreign Missions a Congregational agency founded in 1810. On the ship to India, they chose to exegete the Greek New Testament a bit and decided they should become Baptists, a scandalous act if ever there was one. Indeed, she hurriedly wrote to a New England friend, "Can you ever forgive me, my dear Nancy, when I tell you that I have become a Baptist?" Of their method, she wrote: "We procured the best authors on both sides, compared them with the Scriptures, examined and reexamined the sentiments of Baptists and Pedobaptists, and were finally compelled from a conviction of truth, to embrace the former. Thus, my dear Nancy, we are confirmed Baptists, not because we wished to be, [that's the truth then and now!] but because truth compelled us to be. We have endeavored to count the cost, and be prepared for the many severe trials resulting from this change of sentiment."[2]

And was there a cost. The Judsons went to Burma, began a new mission there and were ever out on a limb in need of funds, friends, and protection from hostile governments. She learned the language quicker than he by spending her time on the streets and in the markets. He was arrested and imprisoned; she bribed the guards to get him food and medicine. He was released and she died in childbirth in 1826 at the age of thirty-seven. But all that began perhaps because she read Jonathan Edwards in a woman's finishing school. Two centuries ago, a woman went out on a limb and charged denominations on the way to Burma. She died there. This summer I had dinner at the Baptist World Congress (2005) with the president of the Baptist Union of Myanmar who says he is the spiritual great-great-grandson of the Judsons. Not all of Ann Hasseltine Judson's children were stillborn.

Now that's what it means to be out on a limb, and that is the heritage that women and men take up as you begin your work here. The limb is out there, but the work begins here.

And then there's Jesus, whose stories are filled with people who venture out on assorted limbs, don't they? Good Samaritans who crawl down into the ditch with the abused one after holier people have "passed by on the other side." A prodigal, even, who finds life so miserable that he decides that he'd just as well make himself vulnerable to the parent whose economic legacy, if not patience, he'd used up considerably. And that impractical woman who spent most of what she had on perfume to anoint the Galilean's head and feet as if he really were the Christ of God.

So Jesus says to them then and there and to us here and now:

---

[2] H. Leon McBeth, *Sourcebook for Baptist Heritage* (Nashville: Broadman Press, 1990) 207–08.

As you go proclaim the message: "The Kingdom of Heaven is upon you." Heal the sick, raise the dead (?), cleanse lepers, cast out devils. You received without cost; give without charge. Provide no gold, silver, or copper to fill your purse, no pack for the road, no second coat, no shoes, no stick; the workers earns their keep.... Look, I send you out like sheep among wolves; be wise as serpents, innocent as doves.... But when you are arrested, do not worry about what you are to say; when the time comes, the words you need will be given you; for it is not you who will be speaking: it will be the Spirit...speaking in you. (Matt 10:6–10;16–20 NEB)

Hearing those words, it is clear that we are all "out on a limb" out there, in the world. We'll try to get ready for that, here, together.

And that brings me to one more story on this day of introductions and orientation. Not long ago I was asked to lecture to Lutheran ministers on pre-millennialism and the *Left Behind* series, that collection of non-fiction novels sweeping the best-seller lists with stories of the "end times," the "rapture," and the terrors of Armageddon. Reading those books, standing in Borders, I decided this: I think I'll write a one-volume sequel called "Stayed Behind," that describes a group of Christians who decided that if the "rapture" came while they were in the world, they'd hold on to a tree (or perhaps a limb) and not go. They'd stay right here. Why? Because they read another story Jesus tells about the shepherd who had 100 sheep and although 99 were safe in "open pasture" as the New English Bible says, he would not rest until the "missing one" (somewhere out there in the wild) was home at last. They stayed behind—no elitist rapture, no safe escape, but out on a limb, with Jesus till the last one comes home. Now there's an exegesis worth pondering, if Jesus tarries and even if he doesn't.

Welcome home to the divinity school. Let's work to get there together. Amen.

# Within Easy Reach:
## Finding (and Not Finding) God in Divinity School

## Dean's Address,
## Wake Forest University Divinity School,
## August 2006

In the 14 August 2006 edition of *Time* magazine, reporter Aparisim Ghosh offers his "Baghdad Diary," a day-to-day description of the most recent of some twenty trips he has made to Iraq since the war began there. As he tells it, the trip with fifty other passengers on the Royal Jordanian flight involved "an hour's uneventful flying over unchanging desert, followed by the world's scariest landing—a steep, corkscrewing plunge into what used to be Saddam Hussein International Airport. Then an eight-mile drive into the city along what's known as the Highway of Death." That day the passengers include the standard crowd—"security consultants," functionaries, reporters, and surprisingly, "three women in white Indian saris with blue borders." He continues:

> The nuns from the Missionaries of Charity, Mother Teresa's order, are a comforting sight. One of them, Sister Benedetta, kindly gives me a laminated picture of the soon-to-be saint and a genuine relic—a microchip-size piece of Teresa's sari. A lapsed Hindu, I'm nonetheless grateful for any and all gifts that purport to holiness; somewhere in my bags are a tiny sandalwood Ganesha, pages of the New Testament and a string of Islamic prayer beads. In Iraq, you want to have God—anybody's God—within easy reach.[1]

"God within easy reach"—what a great image! In fact, throughout the article Ghosh uses considerable religious language to describe his Iraqi journey. That's not surprising, given the religious overtones of this war, more dangerous, more widespread now than when it began, with

---

[1] Aparisim Ghosh, "Baghdad Diary, in *Time*, 14 August 2006, 25.

almost 3,000 US soldiers dead, more than 20,000 wounded and upwards of 100 Iraqis dying daily.

By the way, in the year of our Lord 2006 you came to divinity school. We've graduated an entire student generation since this war started. I hope it will end before you graduate in 2009.[2] That's why the religious language of this *Time* article seems appropriate for our beginning together. What does it mean when a lapsed Hindu uses religious language in an article describing wartime experiences? In war, and in divinity school, for different but parallel reasons, we wonder if God is "within easy reach."

Aren't there folks on and off this campus, perhaps some of our closest family and friends, who sincerely believe that people who go to divinity school—go into "THE MINISTRY"—have God within easy reach? I run into that it in strange ways, annually. Last year when the WFU basketball team forgot how to play basketball, there were a couple of people who consistently pulled me aside before, worse yet after, the games and said something like this: "Padre, we thought that one of the reasons for starting a divinity school was so you folks could "pray us through" to an ACC, if not NCAA, championship." One guy even added: "Didn't Jesus say 'ask and it shall be given you?'" "Yes," I replied, "but Jesus wasn't talking about three point shots." The guy called me a bad name. Here at WFU we are intense about basketball and God; note the order.

Divinity schools are supposed to have God in "easy reach." Better said, I think, is that we have the IDEA of God in easy reach. We talk eternally about God here, wade through biblical and theological studies, church history, practicum's, pastoral care, preaching, and spirituality in search of an idea of God as articulated by others whose insights we embrace and debate with a vengeance. This is graduate school, so reaching for the idea of God must necessarily bear an objective quality that includes critical, scholarly methods of research and analysis. But where God is concerned, one person's objectivity is another person's blasphemy. One person's analysis is another's insult. Like travel to Baghdad, when you start dealing with dangerous ideas, making yourself vulnerable intellectually, spirituality, and psychically, will the god you brought in your suitcases, remain within easy reach or seem farther and

---

[2] The war did not end in 2009.

farther away? I wonder. Perhaps the next three years will punctuate the enduring paradox of the divine: God is with us and apart from us; within and beyond easy reach—the *Deus Absconditus,* as Martin Luther called the God who sometimes seemed so distant, is not always at our beck and call.

Annie Dillard writes:

> The 18th century Hasidic Jews had more sense and more belief. One Hasidic slaughterer, whose work required invoking the Lord (Kosher preparation), bade a tearful farewell to his wife and children every morning before he set out for the slaughterhouse. He felt, every morning, that he would never see any of them again. For every day, as he himself stood with his knife in his hand, the words of his prayer carried him into danger. After he called on God, God might notice and destroy him before he had time to utter the rest, "Have mercy."[3]

We may need some distance from divinity before we can come to terms with the divine proximity.

In the *Time* article, Ghosh says something else: "A lapsed Hindu, I'm nonetheless grateful for any and all gifts that PURPORT TO HOLINESS." Frankly, I thought it might be spiritually impossible to be a lapsed Hindu since with millions of gods and goddesses and multiple ways to escape the cycle of reincarnation, I thought all bases are covered, even lapsedness. Anyway, I love the phrase, "purport to holiness." We do that a lot around here. We purport to holiness, bringing a diversity of pieties to our individual and collective religiosity. Many of you came here because of that, wondering what it would be like to engage persons whose belief systems, liturgical preferences, and prayer practices may be somewhat or considerably different from your own.

In her book, *The Cloister Walk,* Protestant Kathleen Norris recounts the spiritual insights she gained on sojourned at St. John's Abbey in Minnesota. She says that on the feast day of St. Gertrude, the thirteenth-century monastic, she learned this prayer from Gertrude's Fourth Spiritual Exercise: "Deliver me from timidity of spirit and from storminess."[4] If we are going purport to holiness here, perhaps we should try to avoid both the timidity and storminess of spirit. We need the freedom and courage to claim our own voices, speak our piece/peace

---

[3] Annie Dillard, *Teaching a Stone to Talk* (San Francisco: Harper & Row, 1983) 41.
[4] Kathleen Norris, *The Cloister Walk* (New York: Riverhead Books, 1996) 49.

when we choose to do so, but without the cruel rancor of character assassination or arrogance. That is no easy task—claiming the conviction that binds our individual consciences, even when they contradict the convictions of others living and studying around us.

Last Sunday I preached at the Unitarian-Universalist Church in Winston-Salem, out on Robinhood Road. These folks do not have a timidity of spirit. One "U-U" told me: "Unitarians don't sing well at all. They are too busy reading the words to see if they agree with them or not!" At the end of the service, members are invited to come to the front to share joys and concerns with the entire group—it is a cross between a Baptist prayer meeting and a self-help seminar. One woman reported that during last week's church softball game a swarm of bees attacked one of the players, stinging him so extensively that he passed out. Members of the other team, a more evangelical group, asked to have prayer for the man. The Unitarian agreed hesitantly, not given to public displays of piety. Afterwards the Unitarian team agreed: "Well, we guess it can't hurt." They weren't sure about purporting public holiness, but were willing to let those who did have their say and ask God to intervene. They were neither timid nor stormy.

One other thing, Ghosh writes that as he rode into Baghdad, his driver informed him that sixty-six people were killed the day before by a suicide bomber in the Shi'ite neighborhood of Sadr City. Ghosh observes that just "last year that giant slum was the safest district in Baghdad," and comments: "Now I mentally add it to the list of neighborhoods I can enter only at great risk."[5]

And that is my warning to you today as we welcome you to WFU and its divinity school. Some neighborhoods of thought, life and work available to you here should be entered only at "great risk." But strangely, few of those neighborhoods are the same for any of us. Before you leave here in the class of '09, you'll have to enter at least one or two of those dangerous neighborhoods, taking your theology with you.

Ghosh describes the decent into Baghdad, dropping from 30,000 feet almost straight down to avoid possible rocket attack, an act that led one of the most macho of the security officials to start, in Ghosh's words, "whimpering to Jesus." We whimper to Jesus a bit around here from time to time, especially when tests and term papers come due—whimper

---

[5] Ghosh, "Baghdad Diary," 26.

when you write them and we grade them. Let's bring our collective whimpers to the amazing weekly chapel services we share together, a safe place for care and community in our midst. But, as best we can, let's keep our divinity school whimpers to a minimum. They'll be plenty of time to whimper to Jesus out there in the church and in the world, where sin and danger (God, too, I hope) are always in easy reach. Welcome. Peace be with you every one. Amen.

# Knowing Incompletely…

## Dean's Address,
## Wake Forest School of Divinity,
## September 2007

In a story on Gertrude Stein and Alice B. Toklas published in the *New Yorker* last November, Janet Malcom writes: "The instability of human knowledge is one of our few certainties. Almost everything we know we know incompletely at best. And almost nothing we are told remains the same when retold." She illustrates that in specific events from the life of Gertrude Stein, events misinterpreted largely because of the incorrect retelling of detail.[1]

As we begin a new semester at the Wake Forest University Divinity School in the year of our Lord 2007 it is appropriate to recognize the "instability of human knowledge" from the beginning. Gaining knowledge here or anywhere else is difficult, complex, messy, and at times frustrating. Indeed, when it comes to elusive questions about God, Grace, and Gospel, Janet Malcom correctly asserts that, "We know incompletely at best."[2] St. Paul said much the same thing two thousand years ago. Writing to the undeniably dysfunctional church at Corinth he asserted: "My knowledge now is partial…" Then with an eye to an eschatological hope, he added: "but then it will be whole, like God's knowledge of me." (1 Cor. 13:12) As we embark on the new school year at Wake Forest, perhaps we should make a similar confession, affirmed by those of you who begin and those of us who begin again.

Likewise, we should take seriously Malcom's even more sobering comment: "And almost nothing we are told remains the same when retold." As a historian, that is the joy and bane of my existence: I've spent much of my life retelling the stories of dead people, knowing full well that such an effort is shaped (perhaps diluted) by my own

---

[1] Janet Malcolm, "Strangers in Paradise: Life and Letters," *New Yorker* (13 November 2006) 54.

[2] Ibid.

vocabulary (language and rhetoric), my own identity (who I am and who I am not), and my own agendas (implicit and explicit). You do/will too.

We are going to tell you many things in the next three years, and you will tell us things too, on tests, and in papers, sermons, and class discussions. But objectively or subjectively, God knows what the retelling will provoke in all of us. As one of my colleagues remarked years ago, "Goliath got bigger every time David retold that story."

Amid the inevitable uncertainties, however, we can know some things, can't we? We know incompletely, but we can know, even learn, and that is the great hope of what we do here together—explore and extend our knowledge and the ways we might use it in the world. Given that reasonably noble intention, I welcome you here today with three questions worth considering over the next three years (and beyond). *First*, can you contend with texts? *Second*, can you confront the implications of a theology? *Third*, can you cope with memory?

We devour texts around here, and are sometimes devoured by them. We contend with texts on a daily—biblical, historical, theological, homiletical, theoretical, practical, and texts of our own creation. Over the years I've had students who couldn't agree on whether the Bible is inerrant but they were convinced that every word of their term paper was! If you don't know already, then you must learn how to contend with texts biblical and non-biblical, captivating and boring, insightful and infuriating, every class, every day. And the glasses we use to read such texts define your hermeneutic. That's why we wanted to start you off with conversations sparked by an essay about hermeneutics, the methods we use to read and interpret texts. Elisabeth Schusssler Fiorenza gets at this issue brilliantly, I think, in her discussion of the varying glasses—colonialism, feminism, fundamentalism, liberalism, modernism, and postmodernism that impact our response to texts, recognized or unrecognized. She surveys these theories then opts for an "Emancipatory Interpretation" that focuses on "experiences and struggles for survival and liberation in the 'nobodies' who have been marginalized and dehumanized."[3].

Sometimes for the dehumanized, the text is all there is. This summer I attended a wonderful/terrible conference on "Spirituality and the Shoah: Sixty Years After." One of the papers was given by Peter

---

[3] Elisabeth Schussler Fiorenza, "The Ethos of Interpretation," in Rodney L. Petersen, ed., *Theological Literacy for the Twenty-First Century* (Grand Rapids MI: Eerdmans, 2002) 227.

Ochs, Jewish professor at the University of Virginia who has just completed a book on a Talmudic scholar and holocaust survivor who, in his 90s, is one of the world's foremost authorities on the Talmud, that collection of commentaries on the Mishnah, the oral Torah of the Jews. As the rabbi says, "The Talmud is the walking presence of the Mishnah" and Judaism itself was born in the relationship between Torah and Talmud. When sent to the Warsaw Ghetto, the rabbi recalled, "I put my mind inside the Talmud," and lived an "imaginary life." But when sent to Auschwitz, he acknowledged, "My imaginary life stopped." There, he says, "We clung to the book but were consumed by the sword." A Holocaust survivor, he believes that event to be a sign of God's absence from the world. To facilitate human freedom God must have deserted the world and the Jews, leaving it and them to the evil of the Nazis. And God has not returned. But still the rabbi studies the Talmud. Why? Because while God may be absent, the text remains, and we cling to it in hope. Whether you agree with that Talmudic survivor, can you contend with the text, any text, in your own imagination especially in the face of evil and dehumanization?

Second, can you confront the implications of a theology? That is surely a daunting question on your first day since you may not know what theology is, or whether you should have any or not. Others of you may have come here with too much theology and find it needs trimming a bit. Nonetheless, we are a "theology school" we say, so we'd do well to ask, where does theology take us?

For starters, evangelical scholar Alister McGrath says that theology was initially a "systematic analysis of the nature, purposes, and activity of God." By the twelfth and thirteenth centuries, however, the word was also used to describe "the systematic study of the Christian faith at a university level."[4] Frederick Buechner shortens the definition to "the study of God and [God's] ways."[5] Mark Lilla insists that theology is "a set of reasons people give themselves for the way things are and the way they ought to be."[6] For our purposes, perhaps we could say that theology

---

[4] Alister McGrath, *Christianity: An Introduction,* 2nd ed. (Oxford: Blackwell Publishers, 2006) 111.

[5] Frederick Buechner, *Wishful Thinking* (New York: Harper & Row, Publishers, 1973) 91.

[6] Mark Lilla, "The Great Separation," *New York Times Magazine* (19 August 2007): 30.

involves our struggle to know something of the nature of God and its implications for how we believe and act in the world.

Acting on a theology can get you into trouble. Theology, established and dissenting, got Quaker preacher Mary Dyer hanged on Boston Common by New England Puritans in 1660. It informs the Social Gospel of Walter Rauschenbusch and the Prosperity Gospel of Joel Osteen. It shaped Augustine's Just War theory and the pacifist-non-resistance stance of the historic Peace Churches. It formed the postmillennial eschatology of Jonathan Edwards and the pre-millennialism of Billy Graham.

Eschatology, the study of last things, forced me to confront a theology this summer in ways I did not expect. Last month I preached at a church in Asheville where I've been going off and on for more than twenty years. Since it was summer, and since I was just passing through, I decided to preach on eschatology, confronting various theories of Jesus' second coming, especially those in the best-selling *Left Behind* series, including the theory that when the "rapture" comes the "saints" will be snatched out of this world before it gets really, really bad. As a sort of rhetorical devise for making my point I concluded with this: "If the rapture comes any time soon, and I'm entitled, then I'm not going. I'm going to hold on to a tree, or a 'left behind person.' I think I'll stay right here with Jesus who told the story about the shepherd who wouldn't give up till the last sheep got home."

I suspected it would offend some people, and it did, because some told me about it going out the door, and one even wrote me a long, heated letter. But the real surprise came at the very end of the line when a lean, lanky teenager who'd hung around till the last shook my hand, introduced himself, and commented: "I really liked your sermon." Then he added, "And if it's ok, I'd like to stay behind, too, and help the people who are still here." And that's when I got scared. You see, it's one thing to declare your theology, and to use rhetorical devices to make a point, but what do you do when somebody, especially a sixteen year old, bothers to listen and take you at your word. He scared the hell out of me, and my theology. Sometimes people actually believe you and make you confront your theology with them. I hope we get you ready for that terrifying possibility while you are here.

The third question concerns our ability to cope with memory. Memory descends on us around here, born of the intersection of text and theology with our own identities. A few weeks ago, NPR broadcast a terrific story about wine growers in a particular region of France, many of whom are adjusting to the changing climate that seems to be wetter and warmer than in the past. Reflecting on the uniqueness of each year's grapes, one wine maker commented that every vintage has its own identity and to him none ever taste remotely the same. Then he added: "Every vintage I taste brings memory"—of the weather that year, of quality of the grapes, and of "the fights we had while we were growing them."

It will happen here. Texts and classes, research, and responses will touch memories deep within you, of places you've been and experiences you've had, of things you can never let go of and things you've left behind. We are all vulnerable to the ideas and memories we conjure up in every class, so this needs to be as safe a place as possible.

And lest you think the issues of text, theology, and memory are just academic exercises, then consider the observations of Columbia University professor Mark Lilla, published in this week's *New York Times Magazine* regarding the nature of politics and religion currently confronting global society. Lilla writes:

> Today, we have progressed to the point where our problems again resemble those of the 16th century, as we find ourselves entangled in conflicts over competing revelations, dogmatic purity and divine duty. We in the West are disturbed and confused. Though we have our own fundamentalists, we find it incomprehensible that theological identities still stir up messianic passions, leaving societies in ruin. We had assumed this was no longer possible, that human beings learned to separate religious questions from political ones, that fanaticism was dead. We were wrong.[7]

Sober words for Western religionists, and a great challenge for those of us who deal daily with text, theology, and memory.

So welcome to the Divinity School at Wake Forest University. Join us in a quest for knowledge with all the energy you can muster, hoping against hope that St. Paul is right: "For our knowledge and our prophecy

---

[7] Ibid.

alike are partial, and the partial vanishes when wholeness comes." (1 Cor. 13:9 REV)

Great **Text**, don't you think?

# The Four Walls of New Freedom

## Dean's Lunch Address,
## Wake Forest School of Divinity,
## August 2008

In 1942, Thomas Merton, Columbia University professor and citizen of
the world, entered the Trappist monastery of Gethsemani at Bardstown,
Kentucky, a community in which he would remain until his death on 10
December 1968, 40 years ago this winter. I'm rereading segments of
Merton's massive corpus these days in preparation for a lecture at the
Cathedral of All Souls in Asheville on the anniversary of his death. I find
myself returning again and again to this passage of his autobiography,
*The Seven Storey Mountain*, published in 1948, and recounting his entry to
the monastery.

> I rang the bell at the gate. It let fall a dull, unresonant note inside the empty
> court. My man got in his car and went away. Nobody came. I could hear
> somebody moving around inside the Gatehouse. I did not ring again. Presently,
> the window opened, and Brother Matthew looked out between the bars, with his
> clear eyes and graying beard.
> "Hullo, Brother," I said.
> He recognized me, glanced at the suitcase, and said: "This time have you
> come to stay?"
> "Yes, Brother, if you'll pray for me," I said.
> Brother nodded, and raised his hand to close the window.
> "That's what I've been doing," he said, "praying for you."
> So Brother Matthew locked the gate behind me and I was enclosed in *the
> four walls of my new freedom.*[1]

So here you are, tapping on the door of this not-quite monastic-
community. Monks take vows of poverty, chastity, and obedience. At a
Protestant Divinity School we let you choose two out of three! Here you

---

[1] Thomas Merton, *The Seven Storey Mountain* (New York: Signet Books, 1962) 363–64.

are, and we've been praying for you. Welcome to the four walls of your new freedom!

The "walls of freedom" are a strange paradox, for Merton as it turned out, and perhaps for you as well. In welcoming you to a new and much less sanctified environment than the Abbey of Gethsemani, I want to remind you of at least four walls of our freedom here. We have no creed or Abstract of Principles to which faculty or students must subscribe. I doubt if anyone of us knows all the theological intricacies (or quirks) of our colleagues. Academic freedom, freedom of inquiry, freedom of voice, freedom of ideas shape us here, I hope. Nonetheless, there are walls of freedom that inform what we do, create expectations, and guide our life together. Perhaps they aren't walls at all, but gates that open the world and the Spirit.

Here at Wake Forest, the first wall of freedom is **scholarship**. Hence the question: Can you read, write, and think? My God, could Thomas Merton write—that is one reason his written works fill the trade-book stores and Amazon.com. The *Seven Storey Mountain* draws you in from the opening paragraph. Just listen to it:

> On the last day of January 1915, under the sign of the Water Bearer, in a year of a great war, and down in the shadow of some French mountains on the borders of Spain, I came into the world. Free by nature, in the image of God, I was nevertheless the prisoner of my own violence and my own selfishness, in the image of the world into which I was born. That world was the picture of hell, full of men like myself, loving God and yet hating Him; born to love Him; living instead in fear and hopeless self-contradictory hungers.... My father and mother were in the world and not of it—not because they were saints, but in a different way: because they were artists. The integrity of an artist lifts a man above the level of the world without delivering him from it.[2]

Can you hear it? In one short paragraph Merton links his birth with horoscopes, World War I, geography, and Augustinianism. He introduces his life even as he defines the artist in the world. And we are hooked.

So the freedom we offer you within the walls of graduate education is the freedom to read, write, and think. Divinity school is about

---

[2] Ibid.

learning, relearning, extending your ability to read, write, and reflect, reflect, reflect, analyze, analyze, analyze.

During the next three years don't come to me complaining about the work; that is what you came here to do. Complain about the way we teach, about the courses you aren't getting and the courses that don't push you to your limits. Complain about the grades, if you must, but don't complain about the work. Why? Because that is why you are here—to extend your skills as writers, researchers, analysts, and thinkers. Because that is your "calling" as a graduate student, because you owe it to the people who will call you to preaching, teaching, community service, and the unpredictable "care of souls." You owe it to your calling, whatever form it may take, to do the hard work of study.

And by the way, it only lasts three years. You can stand anything for three years. But for heaven's sake (and your own sake) learn to read, write, and think in ways you've not experienced before. That is the first wall of freedom we offer you.

The second wall of freedom of course, is *community*. Hence the question: Can you nurture community here and let community nurture you? Much of Thomas Merton's early writing involves his celebration of and struggle with the nature of community in a monastic environment. In fact, he calls it a "furnace of ambivalence," a great term for community whether found in a monastery, a church, or a divinity school. He writes of his first lessons at monastic community:

> In the Scriptorium, you find a book in the Common Box that begins to interest you intensely: and then someone else gets interested in it too, and every time you want it, you find he has got there first. Out at work you may be put to saw a log with someone who just puts his head down and closes his eyes in prayer and doesn't care how he pulls his end of the saw, so that it continually jams in the log and you have to do five times as much work as usual, with practically no result. ...All this becomes far more interesting when it happens that the same person is the one who coughs down your neck in the choir, and takes the book you want in the Scriptorium, and fails to get your portion [of potatoes] for you at the table...."[3]

Community, monastic or otherwise, is messy, cumbersome, and—like ourselves—sometimes ornery, full of its own theological and

---

[3] Thomas Merton, "Unpublished," from the original manuscript of *The Seven Storey Mountain* in *A Thomas Merton Reader* (Garden City NY: Image Books, 1972) 146.

ecclesial "furnace of ambivalence." We are a small school; we know each other reasonably well, warts and all. We are not a church, but we create churchly moments—intentionally and unintentionally—for community. If a student says to me: "We don't do enough to create community here." I'll listen to his/her concerns but then ask: Do you go to chapel? Do you attend monthly Eucharist? Do you go to community lunches? Do you participate in small group discussions in Art of Ministry? Do you attend a local congregation? Do you seek out professors for conversation in and out of class? Do you ever have a drink with your peers? (Sweet tea or Pinot Grigio, Diet Coke or Red Oak?) Can you let community nurture you here in ways that may shape your life and friendships for the duration?

Merton sums it up for Trappists and for us: "In fact, so marked is the importance given to [communal]...love in our monastic ideal that is occupies a crucial position in the structure of Cistercian mystical theology. The ascent of the individual soul to personal mystical union with God is made to depend, in our life, upon our ability to love one another."[4] Welcome to community; I hope you find it here in the three years that lie ahead.

There is a third wall of freedom found in *spirituality and solitude*. I think the spirituality of this place is dangerous, really, because you are forced to confront the meaning of the ideas you encounter in biblical texts (where will the text take you?), in history (what is the context of your faith?), theology (what concepts keep you awake at night?), ethics (where will conscience take you?), and preaching (how dare you climb up into a pulpit and lay your ideas on anyone?) And, through it all you may ask: Where and what is the Presence of the God? It is a Master of DIVINITY degree, isn't it? So for the next three years are you ready to confront hierophany, those moments when the Sacred appears in the ordinary? Merton writes, and writes, and writes about such hierophanic moments (I do love that word) and their impact on the solitary human being. He is never more eloquent and challenging than in these words from *The Sign of Jonas*:

> God, my God, God whom I meet in darkness, with You it is always the same thing! Always the same question that nobody knows how to answer! I have prayed to You in the daytime with thoughts and reasons,

---

[4] Ibid., 145–46.

and in the nighttime You have confronted me, scattering thought and reason. I have come to You in the morning with light and with desire, and You have descended upon me, with great gentleness, with most forbearing silence, in this inexplicable night, dispersing light, defeating all desire. I have explained to You a hundred times my motives for entering the monastery and you have listened and said nothing, and I have turned away and wept with shame.... While I am asking questions which You do not answer, You ask me a question which is so simple that I cannot answer. I do not even understand the question.[5]

Merton never really tells us what the great question is, and we won't tell you that either, but rest assured, questions will be asked of you that push you from the rational to the non-rational, from left brain to right brain and back again, from objectivity to vulnerability. And in it all there is the solitude of search, your own quest for God and grace, wherever it takes you.

The fourth wall of freedom is relatively easy to articulate but terribly difficult to live out. It is grounded in what I would call *gospel worldliness*, a willingness to take all this freedom of research and reflection with you into the world and do something about it. Thomas Merton channeled the natural worldliness that sent him tumbling to the monastery into a worldliness that looked beyond the monastic walls to the struggles and the pains of human beings worldwide, as evident in his responses to the civil rights movement, the Vietnam War, ecclesiastical renewal through Vatican II, and interfaith dialogue that pursued an uncommon spirituality with Buddhists. In *New Seeds of Contemplation*, Merton wrote of the worldliness of prayer:

I do not mean to imply that prayer excludes the simultaneous use of ordinary human means to accomplish a naturally good and justifiable end.... In fact, a believer should normally do both. And there would seem to be a reasonable and right proportion between the use of these two means [praying and acting] to the same end.[6]

Then, in words that seem frighteningly contemporary, he wrote:

When I pray for peace I pray God to pacify not only the Russians and the Chinese but above all my own nation and myself.... When I pray for peace, I pray not only that the enemies of my country may cease to want

---

[5] Thomas Merton, *The Sign of Jonas* in *The Thomas Merton Reader*, 213.

[6] Thomas Merton, *New Seeds of Contemplation*, in *The Thomas Merton Reader*, 280.

war, but above all that my own country will cease to do the things that make war inevitable.[7]

Lest you think this is mere sentimentality, I would remind you that so outspoken was Merton about our Vietnam incursion, that when he died in a terrible accident in Bangkok the rumor persisted that our own CIA or other intelligence agency might have had a hand in his death.

While you are here, I hope we infect you with a good case of gospel worldliness by which you read the Greek New Testament, Augustine's *Confessions,* Aquinas's *Summa,* Phyllis Trible's *Texts of Terror,* Jurgen Moltmann's *Church in the Power of the Holy Spirit,* and Jonathan Edwards's *History of the Work of Redemption* ALONG WITH the *New York Times,* and, if you must, the *Wall Street Journal,* deciding what it is that brings all those texts together.

So here you are, and like the old monk at Gethsemani opening the door to Thomas Merton and the "walls" of his "new freedom," we welcome you here. What will you bring to us for the next three years? For that we might jump intentionally, if awkwardly, from Thomas Merton to swimmer Michael Phelps, and the best single summary of this amazing human being breaking all records and reason in the Olympics. It comes from British Freestyle swimmer Simon Burnett who says: "I have figured out Michael Phelps. He's not from another planet. He's from the future."[8]

And that is what I would say of you as you begin your graduate work at the School of Divinity, Wake Forest University in the year of our Lord 2008. Some of you may be very weird (I don't know that, I just speculate based on statistical probability), but you are not from another planet. You are from the future. I hope we can help you get back there in the next three years, with wisdom and courage and grace. Amen.

---

[7] Ibid., 281.

[8] Barry Svrluga, "Phelps Now Without Peer," *Washington Post,* 13 August 2008, A01.

# Grace and Blue Whales

## Commencement Address,
## Wake Forest University Divinity School,
## May 2004

Years ago, John Claypool taught my generation of ministers a wonderful phrase for leave-taking: "And as you are going, know this."[1] In his presence and in his honor, I repeat those words to a new generation of ministers, graduates and friends in these brief remarks.

And as you are going, know this: Blue whales have perfect pitch. The sounds of one blue whale may be discerned by another from as far away as two thousand miles away. Human beings cannot hear the sound, except when it is recorded and played at a much slower speed. It is too deep for our ears, but the pitch is perfect, so musicians say. National Public Radio ran a tape of those fascinating sounds recently and they are truly haunting. What they signify we do not know for certain: location, mating, simple identification, or friendly communication. There are an estimated six thousand blue whales living in the world right now, a species pushed almost to extinction by the whalers of the last two centuries.

And Genesis chapter 1 suggests, they got here before us:

> God created the great sea-beasts and all living creatures that move and swarm in the water, according to their various kinds, and every kind of bird; and God saw that it was good. God blessed them and said, Be fruitful and increase: fill the water of the sea, and let the birds increase on the land. Evening came and morning came, the fifth day. (20–23)

Have blue whales been singing to each other since day five of creation? Does God listen for the perfect pitch of their music-language? If

---

[1] The Rev. Dr. John Claypool, IV, was the baccalaureate preacher for Wake Forest University commencement ceremonies in May 2004. Claypool, former Baptist, had recently retired as rector of St. Luke's Episcopal Church, Mountain Brook, Alabama, and was professor of homiletics at McAfee Divinity School, Mercer University. Claypool died of cancer a year later.

they should all vanish, would God long for them in the silence of the deep? The blue whales haunt me now that I've actually heard their songs, and I can't get that longing and beautiful music out of my head. Think about it: they've been singing in perfect pitch across the centuries and we never knew it until now.

So as you are going, know this: The world needs people who will listen to the voices that don't get heard; who are patient enough and open enough, and, yes, vulnerable enough to slow down the screams and shouts and calls for help and hear them where in ways they have perhaps not been heard before—People like yourselves who go looking for perfect pitch where there seems only dissonance and silence. And even when the pitch is not so perfect, you still hear the singing. As you are going, have ears to hear the low, slow sounds all around you that most everybody else will miss.

Also know this, as you are going: The world needs people who will listen below or beyond the sounds that everybody else is hearing. In the cacophony of sounds in the Real World, can you hear anything different? We live in a country that is at war, and in this moment, there are also the sounds of simple names of those people sent home in coffins from that war. The names I list came from the *New York Times* this week: Nicholas Berg 26 (Civilian); Kyle Brinlee, 21 Specialist, Army National Guard; James Holmes, 28, Specialist, Army National Guard; Isela Rubalcava, 25, Specialist, army; Ronald Payne, 23, Cpl, Marines. Hear theirs and other names and know that you go out to a world where people are ending, not beginning their life's service.

And you are not the first, by a long shot. At every graduation, I can't help but recall Dietrich Bonhoeffer's recollection from prison of the number of students at his underground seminary who finished their studies and went off to war and never came back. I remember Jonathan Myrick Daniels, the Episcopal seminarian killed at Hayneville, Alabama, in 1963 simply for working against segregation.

Daniels himself wrote only months before his death: "Reality is kaleidoscopic in the black belt (of the South). Sometimes one's vision changes with it. A crooked man climbed a crooked tree on a crooked hill. Somewhere in the mists of the past a tenor sang of valleys lifted up and hills made low. Death at the heart of life, and life in the midst of death. The tree of life is indeed a Cross."[2]

And I think of Thomas Merton, writing from the Abbey of Gethsemani of the death of his brother in yet another war: "Where, in that desolate and smokey country, lies your poor body, lost and dead? And in what landscape of disaster has your unhappy spirit lost its road? Come, in my labor find a resting place and in my sorrows lay your head."[3] We are at war in what sometimes seems yet another "desolate and smokey country"—two of them to be exact. So can you hear hope beyond and inside the sounds of war where the pitch is always off key?

And if you can, as you are going, I hope you will take with you the other passion of the Christ, leaping out of the Gospels yet, pieces of the story that betray an indescribable passion in the depths of the Word we believe was made flesh. Here are just a few snippets:

"So I tell you her great love proves that her many sins have been forgiven; for where little has been forgiven, little love is shown." Then he said to her, "Your sins are forgiven." The others began to ask themselves: "Who is this, that he can forgive sins?" (Luke 7:47–49)

At that moment his disciples returned and were astonished to find him talking with a woman. (John 4:27)

But when you give a party, ask the poor, the crippled, the lame, and the blind. That is the way to find happiness, because they have no means of repaying you." (Luke 14:14)

He said, "Stop your weeping; she is not dead: she is asleep"; and they laughed at him (well knowing that she was dead). But Jesus took hold of her hand and called to her: "Get up, my child." And she stood up immediately, and he told them to give her something to eat. (Luke 8:52–55)

If one of you has a hundred sheep and loses one of them, do you not leave the ninety-nine in the wilderness and go after the one that is missing until you find it? And when you do, you lift it joyfully on your shoulders, and go home to call your friends and neighbors together. "Rejoice with me!" you cry. "For my sheep that was lost is now found." (Luke 15:3–6)

---

[2] Malcolm Boyd, *Free to Live, Free to Die* (New York: Signet Books, 1967) 41.
[3] Thomas Merton, *The Seven Storey Mountain* (New York: Signet Books, 1962) 396.

These words reflect Christ's other passion, without which his story is exceedingly incomplete. It is a passion for all the sinners lost and found who hurt and bleed and party in our world. That is the passion you take with you, for without it you will never hear the high-pitched cries for help and the low decibels too deep for "normal" ears—passion that will not let you go until at least some of the hungry have been fed, and some of the naked clothed, some of the disabled enabled, and some of the prisoners set free.

So what are you to do as you are going? Jesus says it clear and plain: "Be ready for action, with your robes hitched up and your lamps alight. Be like people who wait for their master's return from a wedding party, ready to let him in the moment he arrives and knocks. Happy are those the master finds awake!"

Take your passion and listen to the world, and perhaps with Teilhard de Chardin, that philosopher, archeologist, priest of another century, you too will daily offer what he called "his Mass upon the altar of the world, 'to divinize each new day.'" Teilhard wrote from the steppes of central Asia: "Since once more, my Lord, ...I have neither bread, nor wine, nor altar, I shall rise beyond symbols to the pure majesty of the real, and I shall offer you, I your priest, on the altar of the whole earth, the toil and sorrow of the world."[4]

So, sisters and brothers, "hitch up your robes" as you are going; keep your lamps trimmed and burning to confront the world's toil and sorrow, singing out in your own perfect or imperfect pitch, the joy and passion of God's good grace. Amen.

---

[4] Annie Dillard, *For the Time Being* (New York: Alfred A. Knopf, 1999) 128.

# The Grace of Wildness

## Commencement Address,
## Wake Forest University Divinity School,
## May 2006

Today feels a little like the *March of the Penguins*, doesn't it? I hope you know that wonderful, Oscar-winning motion picture. It documents the annual pilgrimage of penguins male and female to one of the coldest places on earth where, under the most difficult conditions, they participate together in hatching a new generation of offspring. Today feels a bit like that, not simply because we've dressed up in strange vestments and paraded around together for two or three days, but because we may share more than we think with our penguin cousins on our rapidly faltering planet.

For one thing, like those penguins marching seventy miles from the sea, many of you weren't sure why you came, but something deep inside compelled you to find out. And you did it—you marched here three years ago driven, perhaps, by compulsions too deep for words. We also read in the program this morning the titles of the senior projects and third-year internships you've hatched along the way, documents that profoundly chart the extent and culmination of your work here.

Second, getting a Master of Divinity, like hatching a penguin chick, requires the cooperation of a lot of other living creatures. None of you did this alone, did you? As one of your numbers told me this week, "I don't think I'll ever have a community like the one I've found here during the last three years." Community is necessary to hatch an egg or get a Master of Divinity degree. Third, like the march of the penguins, once this adventure is finished it starts all over again—if not here then in other dangerous places on earth.

Reflecting this week on artic creatures and gospel preachers I remembered a recent *New York Times* editorial in which Verlyn Klinkenborg, a contributing editor to the Sunday op-ed page, explains why he and his spouse live in Vermont, in the country, next to nature.

Amid certain polite reasons, he says, "it really comes down to living as close to *wildness* as we can." Because, he continues, *"the grace of wildness* changes somehow when it becomes familiar."[1]

Klinkenborg tells of the foxes and other varmints that live all around his rural home, and then concludes: "When I say the grace of wildness, what I mean is its autonomy, its self-possession, the fact that it has nothing to do with us. The grace is the separation, the distance, the sense of a self-sustaining way of life."[2]

So go in peace today with penguin and fox alike, and take the grace of wildness with you. Oh, I don't mean the kind of wildness that gets announced on the infamous divlist (email), or the wildness that (so I hear) occurs from time to time at certain celebrations held at one of the "Divinity Houses"—a wonderful but passing sign of justified exuberance and sanctified decadence. Rather, carry with you the grace of wildness that involves a kind of spiritual and intellectual restlessness, an inexplicable bravery in the face of natural and unnatural odds, and the unexpected wisdom of a self-sustaining way of life. I'm not sure what that means for things in the wild, but I think it has implications for wherever we all are headed in the world.

For example, many of us learned this semester that the grace of wildness can be found in what the Jewish philosopher/ecologist Roger Gottlieb (who taught for us this spring) calls "a spirituality of resistance" that, as he says, "directs us toward outer examination, outer transformation, and the pursuit of justice in the world." Indeed, Gottlieb insists that, "To find a peaceful heart...we need to live on **this** earth: fully conscious of what is happening on it, actively resisting that which we know to be evil or destructively ignorant."[3]

So as you are going, carry with you a wildness of heart and mind that compels you to choose some things on this earth to fight against— not everything but some things—things that in a hundred years your denomination, your church, your nation may only then apologize for and repent of. In encouraging this kind of wild resistance, Gottlieb cites an amazing statement from the Danish philosopher Søren Kierkegaard, who wrote that in confronting the needs of the world, "You [know] you

---

[1] Verlyn Klinkenborg, Editorial, *New York Times*, 30 April 2006, 4/13.
[2] Ibid.
[3] Roger Gottlieb, *A Spirituality of Resistance: Finding a Peaceful Heart and Protecting the Earth* (New York: Crossroad Publishing, 1999) 13.

must do something, but inasmuch as with your limited capacities it will be impossible to make anything easier than it has become, you must, with the same humanitarian enthusiasm as the others, undertake to *make something harder."* Thus, Kierkegaard continued: "Out of love for humanity...and moved by a genuine interest in those who make everything easy, I conceived it as my task to create difficulties everywhere."[4]

So take the grace of wildness, the spirituality of resistance, with you into the world, and create a few (more) difficulties, if not everywhere (God forbid), at least here and there where justice is being crushed, war seems constant, and hope is difficult to discern.

Likewise, I wonder if the grace of wildness means that we learn to resist domestication, as University of Chicago scholar David Tracy says, in ancient texts, and also in ourselves. The grace of wildness may compel you to pursue disturbing ideas that will carry you into dangerous territory. It may require you to have self-possession enough to speak the truth clearly, albeit quickly, in a world obsessed with sound bites.

Perhaps you saw such wildness last week on CNN when ex-CIA operative Ray McGovern, friend of James Dunn and Doug Bailey, confronted Secretary of Defense Donald Rumsfeld about the war in Iraq. Rumsfeld was speaking in Atlanta, and several "peace demonstrators" challenged him, yelled at him actually, and were carted off by security guards. But not McGovern, who marched deliberately to the microphone and began to ask probing questions of the powerful Defense Secretary about the way things were and are in our Iraqi incursion. The audience started to boo while security guards grabbed McGovern's arm to pull him from the room. Suddenly the secretary stopped them in words that sum up dissent and democracy all too poignantly in our country these days. "Wait," Rumsfeld said, "give him a second."

"Give him a second." For the life of me I cannot get the hope and sadness of those words out of my head! Whether you agree with McGovern or with Rumsfeld, my question to you is this: Do you have the grace of wildness enough to sound out what you believe must be said to the powerful ones, and are you self-possessed enough to do it when they give you only a second in which to speak? Do you have "the autonomy" and the "grace of distance" to speak the truth clearly with

---

[4] Ibid., 19.

only a second to spare? McGovern did, apparently so well that he engaged the secretary for "a full two and a half minutes," CNN reported, an eternity when truth is on the line.

Remember what Jesus reminded us about the grace of wildness on your arrival here three years ago? He said it best: "But *when* you are arrested, do not worry about what you are to say, for when the time comes, the words you need will be given you; it will not be you speaking, but the Spirit …speaking in you." (Matt. 10:19–20 REB) When the powerful one says: "Give her a second," what will you say? Wild, isn't it? Do not get so domesticated by church or state that you don't know when to speak your conscience even if you are not certain what will come of it.

One more thing: If the grace of wildness is somehow "the sense of a self-sustaining way of life," then I hope you will discover those qualities in what Libba Moore Gray calls a "dancing heart." On a recent family road trip, our daughter, Stephanie, read to us from Gray's book entitled: *My Mama Had a Dancing Heart.* Today let us say that the grace of wildness is also the grace of a dancing heart, the sense of "a self-sustaining way of life."[5]

In the last three years, we've seen a dancing heart in every one of you at some time or another, in the papers you wrote, the causes you espoused, the trouble you've caused, and the ideas that have claimed you. But none of your hearts dance quite the same, not one; they are all unique representations of your personal, communal, and spiritual DNA. Theologically and intellectually, some of you dance the boogaloo, others the electric slide, still others the twist, the two-step, the polka, and even the minuet! A couple of you have dancing hearts, true enough, but because you are Baptist or Holiness, you can't tell anybody!

Perhaps the wildness of a dancing heart keeps us curious, keeps us fascinated, and keeps us exploring ideas, issues, and individuals that cross our paths. But the book title makes a larger point on the very first page: "My mama had a dancing heart, and she shared that heart with me."[6] And in ways often too deep for words you have shared your hearts with us. Now turn them loose out there in the world, touching

---

[5] Verlyn Klinkenborg, Editorial, *New York Times.* See also: Libba Moore Gray, *My Mama Had a Dancing Heart* (New York: Orchard Books, 1995).
[6] Gray, *My Mama Had a Dancing Heart,* n.p.

others, for God's sake, mentoring and teaching them the freedom, the wildness, and the promise that boogies in your blood and in your hopes.

All of which us brings us back to the penguins and their daunting march across an icy wasteland to hatch a new generation in the coldest place on earth. Males and females share the journey, passing the eggs back and forth, walking endlessly to keep their offspring and themselves from freezing. For me, the most amazing scene in the movie occurs when the males and newborn chicks, teetering on the edge of starvation, catch sight of the returning females who have walked seventy miles to bring food in their bellies which they will pass on to their hungry families. (And each female recognizes the sounds of her partner and her newborn.) As the females come over a snowy dune the males see them and let out a collective cry that is at once gratitude for the saving grace of food and the recognition of a realized hope. It is the grace of wildness, summed up in the songs of penguins no less than the words of the Prophet Isaiah:

> Then will the wolf live with the lamb, and the leopard lie down with the young goat; the calf and the young lion will feed together, with a little child to tend them. The infant will play over the cobra's hole, and the young child dance over the viper's nest. They will neither hurt nor harm in all my holy mountain; for the earth will be filled with the knowledge of the Lord, as the waters cover the sea. (Isa. 11:6, 8–9)

Wild words, don't you think? Keep the memory of them in your weary heads and in your dancing hearts, as you are going. Amen.

# Cutting and Keeping

## Commencement Address,
## Wake Forest University Divinity School,
## May 2009

Some two years ago *Bostonia* magazine included a photo of writer/prophet Eli Wiesel in the commencement procession at Boston University where he is Andrew Mellon Professor of Humanities. His academic regalia looked exactly like the one I have on but with one fascinating exception. The two crosses taken from the university's nineteenth-century seal have been removed, and only the outline remains, ghostly evidence of a symbol cut out. Wiesel, Boston University professor, Nobel Laureate, and Holocaust survivor, snipped the cross out of his doctoral gown. As a Jew, he could not carry the cross even in that institutional setting and be faithful to who he is. He cut it out.

And for reasons I cannot fully explain but am about to try, I now think of that photo every time I "suit up" for events at Wake Forest University. In a powerful albeit, wordless way, it compels me to ask what symbols, signs, and sacraments of identity am I carrying, casually or intentionally? And what do I need to keep or cut out according to the dictates of conscience?

Today, at commencement in a divinity school that calls itself "Christian by tradition," Wiesel's vaguely imperceptible but singularly significant act forces me to ask here and now: As YOU are going, what do you cut and what do you keep? Before you came, while you were here, and as you are going, what do you choose to retain and what must you relinquish to be faithful to yourself? Are there some things deep within your mind and heart that liberate you to claim identity, a sense of conscience or conviction that opens some doors to life while closing others? You see, whatever postmodern pluralism means (and you all knew I'd work those words in somehow), it does not mean you won't have to choose—who you are, where you stand, what you mean in the church and in the world. It simply means that you have more choices than previous generations had or recognized.

Today we send you out after three years of biblical-historical-theological-pastoral-homiletical-ethical theory and praxis (amid other things) that we hope helped form you and your sense of vocation—identity—in the world. As you sit here today, I wonder what are the ideas and issues you brought to this program and what you have cut and what you have kept while you were here. I hope we have given you sufficient choices, complicating your lives with appropriate ideas and issues for the struggle. Years ago a student at a seminary where I was teaching came into my office at pre-registration time. "I have to take your church history course," he said, "it is the only time that will work for my schedule. But I am hesitant because I hear you are (1) irreverent, (2) a Catholic lover, and (3) think women should be ordained. And I'm opposed to all that!" "Well," I replied, "if you have to take the class, then would you settle for two out of three?" If we were any good at all during the last three years, perhaps we challenged at least two out of three ideas that were worth keeping or cutting within your own scholarship, your spirituality, or your struggles for identity.

Likewise, whatever you keep or whatever you cut, are you prepared to face the implications of your choices? For a number of years now I have lived in the ethos of seventeenth-century Baptists and have found myself captivated by their courage and their inexplicable anticipation of a pluralistic future. It seems to me they knew that if they retained the vision of what we now call the Free Church Tradition and rejected the prevailing establishmentarian ideology of their times they would have to face the consequences. Indeed, they wrote that reality into their earliest confession of faith from Amsterdam in 1611. In it, they affirmed that they would come together as people of God "to pray, prophecie, break bread, and administer in all the holy ordinances" even if they had no "officers" or if "their officers should be in prison, sick, or by any other means hindered from the church."[1]

I wonder what any of us would do if the congregation calling us to ministry insisted that they would continue to worship God even if we, the ministers, were in prison for conscience sake? And, lest you think that less likely in our pluralistic society, let me remind you that John

---

[1] William L. Lumpkin, *Baptist Confessions of Faith* (Valley Forge: Judson Press, 1974) 120.

Porter, Birmingham pastor whose memory we honor with an award today, went to jail in the 1960s for the sake of civil rights in the South. Last week some Roman Catholics in South Bend, Indiana, went to jail for conscience sake, and last summer I was in Israel with a Mennonite pastor just out of jail for protesting the Iraq War in the halls of the nation's capital. Conscience cuts a wide swath.

Indeed, every generation confronts questions of conscience, seeking the strength to stand, to speak, to hold on, and to not be afraid. Conscience slips up on us, forces us to confront issues and individuals we'd just as soon avoid. When you cut or when you keep the things that really matter, best to know the danger of it.

One other thing: How does your identity inform your discourse, your sense of voice? In a recent interview, Wiesel recalls that he did not speak of his holocaust experiences for a decade after the war was over. Then, he says, he went to see a revered French Catholic writer named Mauriac whom he much admired but who, in his words, "spoke only of Jesus" for most of the conversation. They talked and talked, until finally, Wiesel says:

> When he said Jesus again I couldn't take it, and for the only time in my life I was discourteous, which I regret to this day. I said, "Mr. Mauriac, ...ten years or so ago, I have seen children, hundreds of Jewish children, who suffered more than Jesus did on his cross and we do not speak about it." I felt all of a sudden so embarrassed. I closed my notebook and went to the elevator. He ran after me. He pulled me back; he sat down in his chair, ...and he began weeping. I have rarely seen an old man weep like that, and I felt like such an idiot.... This man didn't deserve that. He was really a pure man, a member of the Resistance.... And then, at the end, without saying anything, he simply said, "You know, maybe you should talk about it.

Wiesel continues: "He took me to the elevator and embraced me. And that year, the tenth year, I began writing my narrative. After it was translated from Yiddish to French, I sent it to him. We were very, very close friends until his death. That made me not publish, but write."[2]

So as you are going, know this: For all the times we talked too much about Jesus, or not enough, I hope we helped you find your voice, the

---

[2] See www.achievement.org/autodoc/page/wie0int-3

framework for a lifelong discourse with the world and a lover's quarrel with the Church of Jesus Christ. Amen.

Part IV

CAN I GET A WITNESS?

COMMENTARY AND REFLECTION

# American Churches:

# A Failure to Thrive?

The Web site kidshealth.org posts this description of a common, cross-generational medical disorder: "Although it's been recognized for more than a century, failure to thrive lacks a precise definition, in part because it describes a condition rather than a specific disease. Kids who fail to thrive don't receive or are unable to take in, retain, or utilize the calories needed to gain weight and grow as expected." It concludes: "This is a general diagnosis, with many possible causes." The term "failure to thrive" (FTT) came to mind this week as the Pew Forum on Religion & Public Life reported that the number of adult Protestants in the US has fallen to around 48 percent, the first time since polling began that American Protestants have not held a religious majority. Press reports suggest that this is no big surprise since Protestant numbers have been dropping consistently for years. More alarming for organized religionists, however, is the dramatic growth of those who indicate no religious affiliation or engagement whatsoever. This figure, for years plateaued at around 7 percent of the population, jumped to near 15 percent in the last five years and now to 20 percent in the Pew surveys. While some of these folks may be "believers and not belongers," pursuing spirituality outside organized religion, a substantial number appear to claim no religious concerns at all. This new data offers further evidence that many trends predicted in American religious life are now realities that exist deep inside the culture, impacting communions across the ideological and demographic spectrum.

Given those developments, the phrase "failure to thrive" offers medical descriptions that seem strangely poignant when applied to ecclesial realities. Pubmed.gov notes that children are not the only ones who can fail to thrive. FTT can "describe a gradual decline in physical and/or cognitive function of an elderly patient, usually accompanied by weight loss and social withdrawal, that occurs without immediate explanation." It concludes that for seniors, "Early recognition and management of FTT can reduce the risk of further functional deterioration"—an equally valid possibility for the church. Hospiceofthecomforter.org offers a dire commentary applicable to individuals and congregations alike, noting that FTT "is caused by multiple chronic conditions and functional losses. Often, the causes of the deteriorating condition are irreversible or sometimes even unidentifiable."

Whether they use the actual phrase, many Christian communions, Protestant and Catholic, Evangelical and Mainline, are increasingly compelled to ask if they demonstrate symptoms of a failure to thrive, hoping such indicators are not yet "irreversible." As disengagement from religious institutions grows, perhaps all American faith communions should examine what it means to thrive in the present and future church. One set of all-too-brief diagnostic possibilities include the following:

First, congregations might begin, not by asking if they are growing, but if they are thriving. Are they engaging their constituents in ways that provide meaning, communal support, spiritual identity, and an invigorating sense of mission within and without? Such churches may thrive even when numerical growth seems less discernable. Thriving churches offer a unique witness in their specific communities.

Second, to thrive, congregations may need to reaffirm their spiritual identity, a sense of who they are under God. This source of identity involves a hospitable traditionalism, offering persons a place to stand, underscoring the significance of their identity in Christ, a people bound together by powerful ideas, rituals, and histories amid a continuing quest for faith, grace, and perhaps even justice. This traditionalism is hospitable when it turns persons outward on the world, not inward on themselves.

Third, a thriving congregation is one that claims its own spiritual, theological, and sociological location and asks how best to energize a constituency and a community. This means continually reaffirming those rites, old and new, which unite and sustain, not only in timeless sacraments of baptism and Holy Communion, but also in traditions formed from particular place and need. It asks, "Who are we in the global church and in our own specific spiritual and geographic setting?"

Fourth, a thriving congregation will be brave enough to confront the wonder and danger of particularism and pluralism. It asks, "What are the theological, ethical, and spiritual foundations that bind our consciences, and how does our calling carry us into the wider arena of ideas, traditions, and world views different from our own, bound together by common concerns and tasks?" Thus centered, individuals are better prepared to engage those different from themselves, connecting when possible for the common good.

Finally, thriving churches might develop certain signature ministries that invigorate their people, engaging them with each other while responding to the needs around them. Such ministries incorporate the church's enduring call to bind up the broken-hearted, creative ways by which specific faith communities attempt to live out their Jesus-identity in the world, thriving with or without a statistical majority.

It has happened before: "... and, breaking bread in their homes they shared their meals with unaffected joy, as they praised God and enjoyed the favour of the whole people. And day by day the Lord added new converts to their number" (Acts 2:47). We can only hope.

# Engaging the Stranger

As Advent turns to Christmas and the reality of a New Year looms, we revisit that often-overlooked, post-nativity saga portrayed by innumerable artists as "the flight to Egypt." Matthew 2:12–14 says that after the Magi left town, Joseph dreamed of an angel who tells him: "'Get up, take the child and his mother and escape with them to Egypt, and stay there until I tell you; for Herod is going to search for the child to kill him.' So Joseph got up, took mother and child by night, and sought refuge with them in Egypt."

As the Holy Family crossed the border into Egypt, "by night," did they become first-century undocumented immigrants? Illegal aliens? Political refugees? Asylum seekers? Whatever else, Joseph, Mary, and the babe were clearly "strangers in the land," an ancient designation that elicited multiple responses from the people of the Bible. In biblical text and culture the Stranger is: 1) An Outsider, not of the tribe; 2) An Other, not like "us"; 3) A Sojourner, merely passing through; 4) An Alien, from some other place; 5) An Enemy, who threatens culture, religion, and security; 6) An Unexpected Presence, sometimes Divine, sometimes Demonic; 7) A "sign of the Kingdom," revealing God's activity with the people on the margins. The Bible offers various, sometimes contradictory, ways for dealing with the Stranger that include exclusion, fear, hospitality, rejection, and genocide, as well as rules for engagement, negotiation of boundaries, evolving relationships, and continuing debate.

Regulations for responding to Strangers appear quickly in the biblical text: "This is the stature for the Passover: No foreigner may partake of it." (Exod. 12:43) "And you must not procure any such [sacrificial] creature from a foreigner and present it as food for your God. Their deformity is inherent in them, a permanent defect..." (Lev. 22:25).

The category of "resident alien" describes a non-citizen who lingers in the land and is not simply passing through. In the Hebrew bible such persons often receive a special response from the "reputable" community in such rules as: "Do not oppress the alien, for you know how it feels to be an alien; you yourselves were aliens in Egypt." (Exod.

23:9) "These are the words of the Lord, deal justly and fairly, rescue the victim from his oppressor, do not ill-treat or use violence towards the alien, the fatherless and the widow... (Jer. 22:3).

At other times the Stranger/Other is an enemy to be confronted: "Thus Joshua took the whole land, the hill-country, all the Negeb, and the land of Goshen.... It was the Lord's purpose that they should offer stubborn resistance to the Israelites, and thus be annihilated and utterly destroyed" (Josh. 11:16, 20).

Sometimes the Stranger is a messenger of the Divine, as in Genesis 18 when "three strangers" show up at Abraham's camp and one of them predicts that Sarah, his spouse, will have a child within the next year. Sarah laughs in his face, realistically, "because I am out of my time and my husband is old." Turns out that the Stranger is actually "the Lord" who asserts that a pregnancy will indeed occur. Sarah gets serious and denies laughing, but the Stranger/Lord insists, "O yes, you did." Sure enough, a child is born and they name him, what else, Isaac (Laughter), and Sarah says, "Everyone who hears this story will laugh with me." Strangers can be prophetic and ironic all at once. In fact, Hebrews 13:2 advises: "Do not neglect to show hospitality, by doing this some have entertained angels unawares."

Jesus confronts the problem of the Stranger in his famous sermon in the Nazareth synagogue: "In Elisha's time," he says, "there were many lepers in Israel, and not one of them was healed, but only Naaman, the Syrian. "These words roused the whole congregation to fury" (Luke 4:27–28). Yet on another occasion, he rebukes the Gentile woman, "a Phoenician of Syria by nationality," who asks him to heal her daughter. "It is not good to take the children's bread and give it to dogs," he declares, but she answers back: "even the dogs under the table eat the children's scraps." Jesus melts under the Stranger's stubborn faith and the child is healed (Mark 7:26–27).

Might these biblical clues inform contemporary dilemmas caused by the Strangers in our midst? All societies have "Resident Aliens" and "Others" whose presence raise questions about culture, tribe, identity, and security. For members of the Body of Christ, radical love demands radical response, evident in Jesus' profound one-liner? "I was a stranger, and you took me in" (Matt. 25:35).

On the eve of a new year, could any of these "hard sayings" inform our own struggles with the Stranger in our midst? Who knows? Surely they are worth considering on the "flight to Egypt" with Jesus, then and now.

# Forgetting To Remember

Last week we moved Lavelle, my mother, to the Alzheimer's Care Unit (euphemistically called "Reminiscence Neighborhood") at her assisted living facility. For the last nine years, two in Texas and seven in North Carolina, she has been in a nursing home, one of the 5.4 million Americans whose illnesses bear the diagnosis of dementia. The Alzheimer's Association says that Alzheimer's disease defines some 80 to 90 percent of all dementia cases. Its early stages include difficulty remembering names, dates, and recent events, as well as deepening depression and apathy. Later on there may be greater confusion, impaired judgment, and mood changes. One slowly forgets how to remember.

My mother has moved through all that, along with other impairments such as the neuropathy that now confines her to a wheelchair. In short, for the last nine years we have watched helplessly as Lavelle and her memory died little by little. Harry Emerson Fosdick, the great twentieth-century preacher, called death the "dark mother, ever gliding near with soft feet." Well, the "dark mother" has been stalking my mother for a long, long time. I date the trauma from the day she called me out of the blue, staring at the picture of me in academic regalia that sat on her mantle and demanding: "Billy, where did you get your PhD? For some reason, I just can't remember!" Days later she had a "spell," as Texans call it, which sent her to the hospital and from there to years of assisted living.

Her neuropathy is so pronounced that both hands remain in a continuously clenched position, allowing the use of only one thumb and forefinger. She has difficulty feeding herself and requires assistance at meals, a reality that precipitated the recent move, perhaps the penultimate phase of her life's journey. Yet her vital signs remain amazingly robust even as the Alzheimer's takes its toll.

Her dementia-dominated memory has erased most of the persons and events of her 93 years. The last of seven siblings, she recognizes me at every visit, although she now believes me to be her brother. She smiles readily, eats sparingly, loves sweets dearly, and retains a good dose of our family's signature obstinacy when asked to do something she does not wish to do. Her caregivers report that they stay out of her way at such times. One said recently: "She's still got a lot of fight in her."

Sometimes scraps of memory bubble up unexpectedly when she speaks of her much-beloved mother and two sisters. Ironically, she has neither forgotten the words to many of her favorite hymns, nor how to cuss when necessary, two enduring traits of many a good Texas Baptist. The deacons from our church take Holy Communion to her each first Sunday of the month, and one of her dear deacon-caregivers told me recently that they often sing the old hymn "Pass Me Not, O Gentle Savior" during those moments. She sings every word from memory. After receiving four painful injections in her hand during a recent doctor's visit, she looked straight at the young physician and commanded me: "Get him the hell out of here." I hope to remain that defiant at 93.

The dementia, the hymns, and the profanity raise nagging questions about life, death, and faith as we all age and learn to play a statistical Alzheimer's roulette. It is amazing, isn't it, the things that stay in our heads? The story goes that on the day before he died John Wesley sat up in bed and sang every word of the Isaac Watts' hymn "I'll praise my Maker while I've breath." Martin Luther, it is said, ever retaining his characteristic earthiness, declared as death neared: "I'll lie down in a coffin and give the maggots a fat doctor to eat."

My longtime friend, the Benedictine monk, Samuel Weber, once told me of the day not long after he was ordained a priest, when he was doing hospital rounds and met a man who identified himself as a "lapsed Catholic," and, manifesting the early stages of dementia, asked how he could be restored to the Church. "What do I need to do, Father?", the man inquired. "Well," said Sam, "you should confess your sins and receive absolution. Then I'll offer you the Eucharist." "But Father," the man protested, "I'm fighting dementia. I can't remember all my sins!" "That's ok," Sam replied, "let's just sit here and talk, and do the best you can."

Each first Sunday, when the deacons bring my mother Holy Communion and read the words of Jesus, "As often as you do this, remember me," the text and the ritual take on a whole new meaning that churches should confront as they care for those who no longer recall the old, old story. Since Lavelle and multitudes like her live in remembrance of no one, even Jesus, then perhaps the church—the community of memory—can believe for her, with her as she sings, and even cusses a little, all the way to the end. Let's all try to remember that, as long as we can.

# Prayers by the Book

In his 1646 work, *The Dippers Dipt,* Anglican clergyman Daniel Featley published a scathing attack on the "Dippers" rampant in England. "Dipper" was an early name for Baptists and their practice of immersion baptism. Featley denounced such baptismal rites, including their implicit promiscuity since "both sexes enter into the River and are dipt...with a kind of spell containing...their erroneous tenets." His other objections included the group's refusal to baptize infants, their failure to distinguish appropriate ecclesiastical boundaries between clergy and laity, and their hesitancy to take oaths or hold public office. He deplored "Dipper" insistence "that there ought to be no set form of Liturgy or prayer by the Book, but only by the Spirit." A repudiation of prayer "by the Book" meant that Baptist conversations with God, public or private, did not conform to the rubrics of the Anglican *Book of Common Prayer* as mandated by the Act of Uniformity, a law approved by Parliament in 1559, the second year of Elizabeth I's reign. Ministers who refused to conform to the *Prayer Book* were liable to fines and sentences of six months in jail for the first offense. A second offense brought a year's imprisonment; a third required a life sentence. Since dissenting "Dippers" refused to abandon their non-conformist practices, even in prayer, they faced continued harassment from the church/state establishment. Religious dissenters could neither pray nor participate in governmentally sanctioned events because their actions did not conform to the political/religious regulations of the day. Their prayers and practices were not "by the Book."

In twenty-first-century America, first amendment-mandated religious liberty may be the order of the day, but praying by or outside "the book" can still create controversy. Such was the case when the Rev. Louie Giglio, pastor of Atlanta's Passion City Church and leader of a movement to eliminate sex trafficking, declined an invitation to offer the benediction at President Obama's second inauguration. Invited because of earlier connections with the President and their shared desire to fight trafficking, Giglio was found wanting for a 1990s sermon critiquing what he called the homosexual "agenda" in America. Concerns over those remarks, and their lack of proper "vetting," led many to question the inaugural committee's invitation to Giglio. In his letter of withdrawal, Giglio acknowledged that while he may at times differ with Obama, "I will continue to pray regularly for the President, and urge the nation to do so."

Giglio is not the first preacher to experience controversy related to sermonic comments and governmental sensitivities. During the 2008 presidential campaign, candidate Barak Obama was forced to distance himself from his longtime Chicago pastor, the Rev. Jeremiah Wright, when that preacher's homiletic critiques of America were broadcast across cable and Internet. Neither Giglio nor Wright, clergymen occupying either end of the political spectrum, seemed acceptable for governmental-occasioned prayer.

Truth is, in pluralistic America, multitudes of clergy from varying faiths have probably prayed or preached outside the boundaries of "the book," disappointing or offending local or national coalitions, left, right, or center. Prayer can be at once comforting, inspiring, and communal, as well as divisive, disturbing, and abrasive. The invocation at this year's inauguration was given by Myrlie Evers-Williams, a civil rights activist whose husband, Medgar Evers, was murdered in 1963 as a result of him fighting against segregation. Yet Evers-Williams's presence was a profound reminder of the prophetic power of prayer in the Jim Crow South half a century ago. The prayer vigils that typified many civil rights demonstrations often generated brutal attacks, actions that galvanized the nation. Although Evers-Williams's inaugural prayer was sensitive and inclusive, in an earlier segregated America neither she nor her martyred spouse prayed "by the book."

These events provoke a very personal response, informed perhaps by the dissenting side of the Baptist tradition. Surely it is time to rethink the way the state co-opts religion for prayer at public occasions, local, state, and national. First, when the government feels it necessary to "vet" my theology before inviting me to pray at a state-sponsored event, I don't need to be praying there in the first place. Whether clergy are liberal or conservative, mainline or evangelical, right or wrong, the government does not need an implicit Act of Uniformity to determine who should pray at its public proceedings. Second, in religiously pluralistic America, prayers at government happenings can no longer be representative enough to reflect all the traditions present throughout the culture. There are simply too many diverse religious communions to accommodate every voice. As a Baptist, I cannot in good conscience participate in such an implicit religious privilege at the expense of other voices, so I won't pray if invited by the state. Third, if public prayer is necessary, might it involve a moment of silence during which individuals can pray as their traditions suggest, or choose not to pray at all? Then only God does the vetting. Finally, these events may compel religious communions to reexamine their own participation in governmental prayer-moments, not because prayer is unimportant, but because it is far too important to be trivialized by political or media establishments.

These ideas are no doubt a minority opinion. Since at least 1646, we "Dippers" have never had much church/state credibility. As Daniel Featley noted, "so the presses sweat and groan under the load of their blasphemies."

# Raising a Lament

Jeremiah said it:
Summon the wailing women to come, send for the women skilled in
    keening
to come quickly and raise a lament for us, that our eyes my run with tears
and our eyelids be wet with weeping....
Teach your daughters the lament; Let them teach one another this dirge:
Death has climbed in through our windows,
It has entered our palaces,
It sweeps off the children in the open air
And drives young men from the streets. (Jer. 9:18, 21NEB)

Millennia later, you'd have thought those words were written for events
at Sandy Hook School in Newtown, Connecticut, after twenty children
and six adults died in a horrific massacre perpetrated by a man-child
gone mad. Hearing the wails that erupted as President Barak Obama
read the names of the dead in a community worship service on the
Sunday evening after the murders, the ancient words of both Jeremiah
and Matthew linked Herod's "slaughter of the innocents" in first-century
Palestine with twenty-first-century Connecticut: "A voice was heard in
Rama, wailing and loud laments; it was Rachel weeping for her children,
and refusing all consolation, because they are no more" (Matt. 2:18). The
same scriptures that offer hope also describe the reality of evil that can
overtake any of us, any time, any place.

   You can buy a Bushmaster AR15 semi-automatic rifle at Wal-Mart.
That was the weapon of choice for the twenty-year-old murderer Adam
Lanza, a gun legally licensed to his mother, who was the first of his
victims. The Bushmaster AR15 was apparently the weapon used by
Jacob Tyler Roberts earlier the same week when he killed two people in a
random shooting spree in an Oregon shopping mall. It was the firearm
used by James Holmes in his attack in the movie theatre in Aurora,
Colorado, earlier this year, killing and wounding multiple victims. The
gun remains available in at least 1,700 Wal-Mart stores, so *The Nation*
reported. Such weapons, adapted to rapid-fire ammunition clips, can be

secured at places as basic to American culture as Wal-Mart or national gun shows. Gun shows apparently account for 40 percent of firearm purchases in a context that requires little or no immediate background check.

Were these gun-purchasing venues to blame for the twelve mass murders that took the lives of 88 people in the US this year alone? Debates over that question rage. But the general silence of national leaders in response to earlier shootings was deafening until the inconsolable laments of families were heard by millions who watched the service in Newtown on the third Sunday in Advent, 2012. Since then, voices as varied as New York mayor Michael Bloomberg, a longtime proponent of increased firearm legislation, and conservative MSNBC commentator Joe Scarborough have taken up the lament with calls for more strenuous laws for sales of automatic weapons and multi-shot ammo clips. Confessing that "the ideologies of my past career were no longer relevant" after the Newtown debacle, Scarborough declared that the Constitution does not allow "gun manufacturers the absolute right to sell military-styled, high-caliber, semi-automatic combat assault rifles with high capacity magazines to whoever the hell they want."

Other analysts across the ideological spectrum now suggest that as a result of the Newtown slaughter the "national psyche is changing" and that new attention must be given to issues that include: 1) firearm regulation and use; 2) increased resources for responding to the mentally ill; and 3) strategies for confronting the "culture of violence" evident in certain video games, films, and music. Conventional wisdom and past experience suggests that dealing with even one of those concerns will be complex, controversial and laborious. Nonetheless, Newtown seems to have created a will for it.

What might this mean for people of faith? Perhaps clues for faith-based responses were evident in the community worship broadcast from Newtown that Advent Sunday evening. In profound ways it revealed that communities of faith representing multiple religious heritages and theological-cultural viewpoints could come together in a desperate but concerted effort to console the inconsolable. Representatives of those diverse religious communions reached deep into their holy books, prayer traditions, and pastoral resources to offer immediate presence and sustained care. Catholic, Protestant, Baha'i, Muslim, Jewish ministers, they were the people "skilled in keening" (mourning), who knew how to raise a lament, to give voice to the collective grief of an inconsolable people.

The tragedy at Newtown means that faith communities in every town and city must prepare as intentionally as any other set of "first responders" before firearm violence descends upon them. Representatives of religious traditions need extended strategies to confront the enduring lament of families who will struggle with grief long after the news crews have departed and the candlelight vigils have gone out. This is ministry of presence for the long haul.

The slaughter of the Newtown innocents compels changes—social, legislative, and cultural. Yet if recent history is any indication, other times of horrendous violence probably lie ahead. When death climbs in through our windows, will we be "skilled" enough to respond to the inevitable laments?

# Rescuing Advent from Christmas

In 394 CE, the Spanish nun Egeria visited Holy Land sites, participating in the church's great liturgical moments from Epiphany to Easter. She kept a wonderful diary of her exploits that included this experience in Bethlehem's Church of the Nativity on Tuesday, 5 January 394: "I was fortunate enough to be granted permission to pass through the underground passage in the outer north wall into the very cave itself. By what words, with what voice, can I describe it? That manger too wherein the babe wailed is better honoured by silence than by imperfect speech. In this little nook of the earth the Founder of the heavens was born; here He was wrapped in swaddling clothes, beheld by shepherds, shown by the star, adored by the wise men. And as I knelt there...with mingled joy and tears..."

Leaving the church for the "village" of Bethlehem, Egeria found that "the ploughman...sings Alleluia; the "perspiring reaper diverts himself with chants," and the "vinedresser sings...the songs of David." She concluded: "I was so uplifted, so that the evening came before I was aware of it." Returning to Jerusalem on January 6, she began Epiphany by confessing: "After we had rested from the fatigue of our devotions on the night before, we all gathered at eight o'clock in the Great Church which is in Golgotha."

A footnote in my copy of Egeria's diary reports that toward the end of the fourth century, St. Jerome—who lived in a cave under the Church of the Nativity—complained that the "manger of sunbaked mud," supposedly the original, was replaced by a silver one. Is that when Christmas started going downhill?

Reading Egeria after watching scenes from this year's Black Friday rituals—mobs of people trampling, fighting, cussing each other—it dawned on me that this "Christmas season" we are a hell of a long way (theologically speaking) from "that little nook of the earth."

So here's a proposal for the postmodern church, toward dialogue if not implementation: Let's give up on "the Christmas Season." Let's admit that the mall-mobbing, gift-obsessing, economy-benefitting, Culture-Christmas that begins with Black Friday, continues on Cyber

Monday, and culminates in the disillusion of January refunds, has won the day, and accept that as a socio-economic reality. But let's not confuse the "Christmas Season" with faith, for God's sake.

Let's also confess that if Christians continue to act like the "Christmas Season" has anything to do with the Jesus story then we deserve what we get. Let's run from current culture-bound public forms of Christmas (including carols on the mall sound system), and embrace the season of Advent as fast as we can. Let's make Advent—the four weeks of prepping for Christ's "coming" into the world—the contemporary church's witness against the current "Christmas season" hype. Many churches do that already; but let's all get serious about it.

Wikipedia [Note to students, Wikipedia is not acceptable for academic articles which this is essay is not!] reports that in a sermon given around 386 in Antioch, John Chrysostom ("Golden-mouthed") affirmed December 25 as the date of Jesus' birth. His Biblicist literalism linked biology and theology with elaborate speculation that Jesus' conception (Luke 1:26) occurred in the sixth month of Elisabeth's pregnancy with John the Baptist (Luke 1:10–13). This he linked to John's father Zacharias's participation in the Day of Atonement during the seventh month of the Hebrew calendar… (Lev. 16:29, 1 Kings 8:2), which would mean Jesus was conceived between September and early October. (Whew!) Apparently dates like May 20, April 19, and January 2 were at some point considered Christmas possibilities. December 25 was also a popular celebration of birth of the "Sol Invictus," the "Invincible Sun" by various groups including the Mythra sect. The Western Church ultimately chose December 25.

Advent is first mentioned in certain sixth-century materials as a time of Christmas preparation that paralleled Lent, with fasting and meditation on the incarnation of Jesus Christ. Advent soon became a part of the Christian Year, an annual retelling of the Jesus story to ancients who, like current postmoderns, had limited knowledge of gospel details. Unlike Christmas, Advent still belongs to the church, four weeks focused on hope, peace, joy, and love.

So let's all take the pledge: For Christians, nobody gets to Christmas without going through Advent. Nobody reads the phrase "and she brought forth her firstborn son and wrapped him in swaddling clothes and laid him in a manger" (Luke 2) who hasn't previously read Mary's prophetic warning: "the arrogant of heart and mind God has scattered, but the humble have been lifted up; the rich sent away empty, but the hungry have been filled with good things" (Luke 1).

With Egeria, let's celebrate "the fatigue of our [Advent] devotions," not the exhaustion of shopping till dawn. Let's leave Santa at the mall and put nativity scenes in our front yards. But be careful. Our family considered putting a nativity scene in the yard as this year's Advent witness, but since two "Obama for President" signs were stolen from that space during the recent election, we decided to keep the nativity indoors. If people in Winston-Salem, North Carlolina, will steal Obama signs, they'll steal the Baby Jesus too, given half a chance. Even if the manger isn't silver. Alleluia.

# Vanishing Mountains

Zeb Mountain, Turner Spur, Peters Knob, Big Fork Ridge, Millard, Cow Knob, Cherry Pond, Payne Knob—those are but a few names of the more than five hundred mountains from Kentucky, West Virginia, and Virginia that have disappeared from the face of the earth, never to return. Psalm 121 in the King James Bible begins, "I will lift up mine eyes unto the hills." Not any more, at least in certain segments of Appalachia.

Master of Divinity student Greg Griffey, a son of Appalachia, writes in his senior thesis at Wake Forest University School of Divinity:

Both strip mining and mountaintop removal are employed by coal companies in Appalachia to gain quick and cheap access to underground coal with minimum labor costs. Strip mining strips the surface of the earth, along with any vegetation it sustains. Mountaintop removal goes a step further by literally detonating whole mountaintops, leveling them to flat rock. Both methods disfigure physical landscape, pollute water and streams, and destroy the natural environment. Both practices are the most recent and most permanent of a long line of Appalachian labor and resource exploitations that have driven "progress" in the United States for centuries.[1]

Some things are just plain wrong. And mountaintop removal (MTR) is just plain wrong. It may have approval from 1) certain corporations; 2) congress; 3) local municipalities; 4) some mountain folk, but it is still just plain wrong. Indeed, MTR is fast becoming a ghastly symptom of what is wrong with America: an abiding loss of identity, politically, economically, communally, and spiritually.

In his prize-winning volume entitled *Uneven Ground: Appalachia since 1945,* Appalachian scholar Ron Eller comments:

Appalachia endures as a paradox in American society in part because it plays a critical role in the discourse of national identity but also because the region's struggle with modernity reflects a deeper American failure to define progress in the first place.... We *know* that Appalachia exists

---

[1] Greg Griffey, "Effacing Storied Identity: Mountaintop Removal in Appalachian Place, Biblical Faith and Theology," (M.Div, Wake Forest University School of Divinity, 2011).

because we need it to exist in order to define what we are not. The notion of Appalachia as a separate place, a region set off from mainstream culture and history, has allowed us to distance ourselves from the uncomfortable dilemmas that the story of Appalachia raises about our own lives and about the larger society.[2]

In her groundbreaking study, *Appalachian Mountain Religion,* Deborah McCauley writes that Appalachia harbors a unique form of Protestantism born of "oral tradition," the "centrality of religious experience," and the "reality of the *land.*" McCauley concludes that, "the mountainous terrain that is the Appalachian region has had enormous impact on its character, its texture, and its religious values."[3]

Building on the work of Eller and McCauley, Greg Griffey insists that, "By destroying the mountainous landscape of a geographical region formed millions of years ago, we are now effacing, and thereby choosing to forget, storied identities that have beckoned habitation, provided navigation through space, and evoked senses of rootedness in the mountains for thousands of years." His thesis explores "the interconnectedness of place, the environment, and religious and cultural thought," a communal network challenged by mountaintop removal in "tangible and intangible" ways.[4]

These studies suggest that a dramatic symbol of the loss of American regional and religious identity is found in the environment. This clear and present danger has reached crisis proportions as forests disappear, streams and creeks are crammed with sludge, and mining continues to make the landscape bleak. But in twenty-first-century Appalachia, perhaps the most sobering reality is the loss of the mountains themselves. Through MTR techniques, mountains formed more than five million years ago have disappeared forever, their non-coal contents tossed into valleys, creek beds, and hollows with devastating effect. Eller writes that "with few exceptions" the promised economic benefits of mountaintop removal "never materialized, and communities were left with miles of deserted, treeless plateaus, poisoned water tables, and a permanently altered landscape."[5] If McCauley is

---

[2] Ronald D. Eller, *Uneven Ground: Appalachia since 1945* (Lexington: University Press of Kentucky, 1908) 3.

[3] Ibid., 6–7.

[4] Griffey, "Effacing Storied Identity."

[5] Ronald Eller, *Uneven Ground,* 227.

correct that Appalachian religious experience was shaped in part by the "reality of the *land*," then the culture and religion of Appalachia may be vanishing because the mountains are vanishing. Appalachian religious communities embody the value and fragility of sacred space, the struggle to maintain it, and the identity crisis that inevitably results when it slips away.

Appalachians discovered faith up hollows, on mountaintops, by cold clear streams, and in deep lush valleys. They've spent years renegotiating that faith with strip mines and strip malls, slag pits and condominium complexes, polluted rivers and manhandled mountains. They mirror the world moving as fast as it can to undo sacred space across the globe. Today, the creature, not the Creator, "makes waste mountains and hills and dries up all their herbs"; the creature, not the Creator "makes the rivers islands and…dries up the pools," (Isa. 42:15), questionable conduct with no end in sight. So as the mountains continue to crumble, perhaps we'll have to hedge out bets on Isaiah 72:3: "May hills and mountains provide your people with prosperity in righteousness." Maybe not, O Lord, maybe not.

# Who are the "Nones?"

As noted earlier in this space ("Here Come the 'Nones,'" *Associated Baptist Press*, 30 December 2010), recent polls give evidence of a dramatic increase in the number of Americans who self-identify as having no religious affiliation—statistics up from 7 to close to 17 percent in the last few years. These individuals, identified as "nones" in the new book, *American Grace*, by Robert Putnam and David E. Campbell, require serious attention from persons who remain engaged in religious communities. If the nones are increasing, and apparently more people are at least willing to claim that designation, then who are they and what might their identity suggest for the church? Putnam and Campbell offer some insightful initial responses drawn from a studying a variety of polls:

While drawn extensively from a "post-boomer" constituency, nones actually reflect a profile similar to other Americans educationally and socially. There are slightly but not significantly more males, whites, and non-Southerners, they do not represent a clear social anomaly.

While religiously non-affiliated, they are largely unwilling to identify as completely "non-religious" atheists or agnostics. This may reflect the influence of the "spirituality movement" on individuals who pursue religious reflection, contemplation and literature but not in traditional corporate settings.

Nones apparently come from both religious and non-religious family backgrounds. While many were not reared in religious communities, a certain portion was and they too have chosen to disengage.

Nones tend to reflect ideas and values that are somewhat left of center on the ideological scale and their rise parallels the expansion of the Religious/Political Right. Many are younger Americans who, as one study has shown, see religion "as judgmental, homophobic, hypocritical, and too political" (121).

In one of their most intriguing observations, Putnam and Campbell conclude: "Because the rise of the new nones was so abrupt, this increase seems unlikely to reflect secularization in any ordinary sense, since theories of secularization refer to developments that transpire over decades or even centuries, not just a few years" (127). Blaming secularism won't account for the dilemma. This observation leads the authors to ask whether the increase of nones is at least in part evidence of a "backlash against conservatism."

Backlash, however, may not be the only appropriate way to describe the nature of "none-ness." Perhaps the new nones are another evidence of the new pluralism, a reality that religious communities across the theological spectrum need to confront, and soon. The new pluralism means that religious and non-religious diversity is so extensive, so widespread that those who challenge it can sound more like bigots than faithful dissenters. In fact, for many people (apparently some of the nones) what sounds like conviction in many communities of faith may appear as bigotry when such rhetoric enters the public square. The new pluralism means that sectarian declarations regarding ethics, dogma or religious experience may turn persons away as readily as it draws them in. It may indicate that for many people the religion-culture wars are ending not with a bang but with a whimper. Religious communities right and left have declared themselves, and a certain segment of the population has gotten the message, quietly choosing to walk away. That reality may be a factor in yet another poll that appeared in the last few weeks. This one, from the Gallup organization, indicates that while 54 percent of the Americans surveyed believe that religion is important in their lives, some 70 percent suggest that "religion is losing its influence in American life," one of the highest such figures in the history of Gallup's studies. While this data is not necessarily dire—these attitudes fluctuate greatly in American life—when combined with the statistics on the nones, it should at least be sobering to religious groups large and small. Whatever else, it suggests that a distinct religious identity is becoming increasingly less normative in American life.

Does all this mean that faith communities should cease addressing the larger culture on the basis of conscience and conviction? Of course not, but it does mean that they should know where their declarations and actions may take them in terms of popular perception and public response. It may also mean that as religious pluralism sweeps every corner of the culture, there can be no real "mainline" American religion. Every faith tradition has the freedom to articulate its vision (dare we say its "witness?") publicly and privately, even as it is forced to recognize that no one religious communion can establish, demand, or secure culture-dominance. Such pluralism suggests that the voices of religious institutions and individuals may be both present and limited in the marketplace, a reality that is hitting many Protestant groups hard. Ultimately, however, the nones may be a blessing in disguise, compelling the church to revisit, review, and recover the meaning and method of its primary witness in the world.

# Index